POETRY
now

ONE STEP CLOSER

Edited by

Joanne Baxter

First published in Great Britain in 2000 by
POETRY NOW
Remus House,
Coltsfoot Drive,
Woodston,
Peterborough, PE2 9JX
Telephone (01733) 898101
Fax (01733) 313524

All Rights Reserved

Copyright Contributors 2000

HB ISBN 0 75430 883 9
SB ISBN 0 75430 884 7

FOREWORD

Although we are a nation of poets we are accused of not reading poetry, or buying poetry books. After many years of listening to the incessant gripes of poetry publishers, I can only assume that the books they publish, in general, are books that most people do not want to read.

Poetry should not be obscure, introverted, and as cryptic as a crossword puzzle: it is the poet's duty to reach out and embrace the world.

The world owes the poet nothing and we should not be expected to dig and delve into a rambling discourse searching for some inner meaning.

The reason we write poetry (and almost all of us do) is because we want to communicate: an ideal; an idea; or a specific feeling. Poetry is as essential in communication, as a letter; a radio; a telephone, and the main criteria for selecting the poems in this anthology is very simple: they communicate.

CONTENTS

Britain In The Third Millennium	Carol Frankland	1
New Beginnings	Lesley-Ann Curdy	2
Past, Present Or Future!	Jeannette R D Jones	3
2000 Anno Domini	J F Munro	4
Future Full Of Strife	S Mullinger	5
Have No Regrets	Frances Falvey	6
Oh Lucky Man	John Heron	7
Sunrise 2000	Elizabeth Maria Rait	8
A Time Of Grace	Eileen Pennell	9
Looking Forward, Looking Back	Pat Allington Smith	10
A Millennium Plea	Niall Mclaren	11
Alternative Cargoes	Mick Nash	12
Ever Hopeful	Phyllis M Dunn	13
Thy Kingdom Come	Marian Lacy	14
Friendship	P Fisk	15
A New Planet	Maria-Louise Stephens	16
Cenotaph	Michael Wilson	17
Looking Forward	Zahida Darr	18
Do We Have To Sign For This	J Brown	19
Michaelmas Daisy Time	Anne Sanderson	20
Reminiscence	Ann Odger	21
Thoughts Of The New Millennium	P G Clarke	22
Breakaway	Susan Lewis	24
Exodus	Philip Mee	25
Out Of The Mist	Joanna Carr	26
Who Cares?	M Lesley Nicholls	27
2000 - Our Children's Legacy	Angela Wakefield	28
Time Honoured Christendom	Marion Monahan	29
A Grandmother's Thoughts For The Next Millennium	M McCoy	30
Britain In The Third Millennium	Mark Lello	32

Upside Down And Spinning Round	Kurt Perry	33
We're In The Year 2000	N J Ball	34
Millennium Shame	Gilbert	35
This Is The Time	Sarah Payne	36
Wessex	Margaret Boles	37
At The Eventide Home, Scalloway	Stella Shepherd	38
Britannia Weeps	Maxwell Anderson	39
To Be Or Not To Be!	Maureen Astley-Mullen	40
Moving On	Paul R Giannandrea	41
A Perfect World	Kath Barber	42
2000	Jessica Preston	43
Third Millennium	Alfred Warren	44
Looking Back	Robina Karasek	45
My Memories	Alan Rogers	46
The Pits	Janet Follett	47
Goodbye To The Twentieth Century	Susan Glyn	48
The Millennium At Last	Kenneth Jackson	49
Untitled	Terry Williams	50
Walking On The Right Side	Les J Croft	51
Power To A Ninety Year Old	Meg Pybus	52
Millennium's Mirth	R F Short	53
Future Hopes	Reg Morris	54
What Have We Done	John Hewins	55
If Only Now We Find The Way To Love!	Peter James O'Rourke	56
Distant Times	Foy Kennedy	57
The Future	Stella Van Onselen	58
All It Takes	Lionel Stanbrook	59
Looking Forward	Terry Daley	60
New For Old	M Baker	61
The Next Millennium	Rachel Greener	62
The British Ride	Stephanie Mottram	63
Our Future!	Eileen Ayres	64
Children At War	Elisabeth Ware	65
Greetings	Anthony Maccini	66

You Do Not See Yourself As You Are	Sue Moules	67
Millennium	Irene Patricia Kelly	68
Sacred Horse's Ghost	Paul Belshaw	69
Second Chance	Peter Davies	70
Homeless	Caryne Crane	71
There Was A Time . . .	Alan J Hedgecock	72
Past, Present And Future	J M Gardener	73
A Double Edged Sword - In The Hands Of Time	Christina B Cox	74
Forty Years Ago I Was Seven	Michèle Umpleby	75
The March Of Time	Ruth Daviat	76
The Third Millennium Race	Robert Lumley	77
Question For The London Eye	Sandra Game	78
3rd Millennium - The Outcome	C Carey Jones	79
Our Time	Olive Noad	80
Two Thousand Years	Arthur W Gilliland	81
Millennium Hope	D Hayter	82
Untitled	Charles Wayne Leadbeater	83
History Tomorrow	Cardinal Cox	84
Millennium Dreams	Trisha Buchanan	85
Through The Eyes Of Love	Margaret Suffolk	86
The Millennium	Dianne Pike	87
2030	C D Tubbs	88
Baldheaded Into YK3	Roger N Colling	89
Waiting For The Ghost Of Sunrise 2999 CE	Steve Sneyd	90
2000 Years	Marion Joyce	91
Normal Life '99	Rhys Thomas	92
Death In The Final City	M Stone	93
Let It Go	Elizabeth E. Picard	94
The Washing Machine	J Stuart	95
Millennium Saturday	A S C Smart	96
As I Look Back	Irene Keeling	97
Nostradamus Said (?)	Anthony Manville	98
Millennium	Elaine Johns	99
The Breaking Day	S V Batten	100

My Thoughts For The Millennium	Mary Hellard Eastwood	101
What Does It Mean For You?	Timothy Paton	102
My Hopes For The New Millennium	Kirsty Sellar	104
H O P E	J Daintree	105
Millennium	Ann Linney	106
A Vision Of The Future	J Paton	107
Looking Forward	Jenny Brownjohn	108
Arrows	Freda Hendry	109
Great British Oak	Angeline Laidler	110
Y2K	Sheila Colling	111
Millennium	L J Edwards	112
High Street 2100	Paul Edwards	113
The Children Did Play - 1930's	Gloria Aldred Knighting	114
We Who Dream	Sandy Lunoe	115

BRITAIN IN THE THIRD MILLENNIUM

Our beautiful blue world swinging and turning endlessly in space.
The sun rising mysteriously over it, fingering his rays
Across the atolls, above the mountains, cities, villages and farms,
Shining upon the peoples of this incredible globe
In all their rich variety and versatility.

Midnight, and there we were praying, singing, laughing, dancing
And, above all, hoping.
In that fleeting second at the end of two thousand years
Each one of us grasped a moment of significance.
The surge of peaceful joy crept round the world
Over all its peoples - and most of us sighed with hope.

Discussing our insights two weeks later
Many agree that in that richest of moments
This lovely world of ours touched an experience,
A common cord - a thread that maybe some of us
Will seek to follow towards a worthwhile future
For all those millions who long to love and to be loved,
To have food and health and a land fit for their children.

Let us pray that the light of that special second will shine in us
And in all who care in this great land of ours
So that we may help to establish trust and hope
Between all the people we've just seen,
Not only in our own villages, streets and towns, but in every part
Of this magnificent blue world whereon we dwell together.

Carol Frankland

NEW BEGINNINGS

A mere moment,
A tick in time,
Two clock hands together
Make, for a new beginning.

Fresh starts;
Resolutions to be made,
Promises to family and friends.
The start of something new.

New year,
New date,
New time,
New millennium.

There's been;
No mistakes,
No arguments,
No deaths,
Nothing,
Yet!

The year can only be
What you and others make it,
Good or bad.
Don't dream it,
See it,
Do it,
Live it,
And be happy!

Lesley-Ann Curdy

Past, Present Or Future!

I wonder what the children of tomorrow will see?
Will they be as lucky - or luckier than me?
I've lived through war, conflict and strife,
But, there's been many 'marvels', during my life!

A man can have breakfast in his home, about nine -
Then by the evening, in New York he'll dine!
The highest of mountains has been climbed by man.
The fastest of races, he also ran!

The higher, the lower, the longer, or wide -
Nothing by man, has not yet been tried!
New barriers they break - new records they set.
Such news - topping headlines, daily we get!

For travellers and explorers of our future race
What epic challenge, can they hope to face?
What future achievement, have we left undone,
Yet to be conquered by some future son?

No doubt in their searching, they'll find something new,
Something man previously, had not thought to do!
Like all generations that came on before,
They'll push themselves further, to do even more!

When you read of past days, and the men long ago,
Pages of history, all go to show -
That man is a stepping stone, along life's stony way,
Bridging the gap - right up to today!

So what path have we laid for the children ahead?
On what perilous journey, will they bravely tread?
There's nothing to give us a signal or sign -
The answer is only, in the fullness of time!

Jeannette R D Jones

2000 ANNO DOMINI

The embryo of Mother Earth, the Earthite
Now a child of the cosmos, stood at the fields of probability
The Earth time story to be told.
For the time trail breaking, or was it part or the same time that had preceded?
The Earthite knew that it was not, but only part of the infanatum and the approaching millennium.

Earth time story
For the balance of the universe is perpetual
The seasons of this planet Earth, shifting but constant
The existence of the Earthite is dubious
For like a flash of lightning in the darkest night.
We are briefly seen, then forever gone.

For this galactic spheroid in the inky blue of space
Has upon its surface a human race
This marble globe of life
Seems at a distance peaceful, more closely observed, is in reality
Torn asunder by war and strife.

Shared with the other Earthites
Whales, dolphins, tigers, butterflies and you
Shed a tear, shed your tears, Earthites kill the whales, dolphins, tigers and butterflies
Earthites kill each other too
Can we see, will we see?
Will we be here for the next millennium on this coloured globe of life
Sustained in the void of perpetuality blue
Shed a tear, shed a tear, for oblivion total, could be near for the Earthite
Who is also me and you.

J F Munro

FUTURE FULL OF STRIFE

Suppose the future will be an exciting place to live,
But the speed at which changes are being made, something has to give.
In Victorian times I would not have been out of place,
My fear of future developments I must try hard to face.

But I do wonder what will happen to family life,
Because latest technological age seems full of strife.
Although we have new machines to help with the daily grind,
Say we do not appear to have more leisure time I find.

S Mullinger

HAVE NO REGRETS

The past is gone - have no regrets,
The dreams were sweet,
The triumphs, too,
The failures? What they did for you,
Will make or break the now and later.

Now is the perfect time to say -
I learnt a lesson yesterday.
The past is gone,
The present's here,
The future holds the key for you
To start the dreams and glories too
From the failings of yesterday.

Frances Falvey

OH LUCKY MAN

Oh lucky man
One foot on the stars
One in hell.
Which way you'll step
No one can tell.
Oh lucky man
Do you look to the past
With its blood and war
Or take the path to the future
That promises so much more?
Oh lucky man
Cushioned from evolution
By the technology you dreamt
Will you evolve emotionally
To adapt to your environment?

John Heron

SUNRISE 2000

There is a little angel
Skipping her rope through time,
Crack! goes the rope
At the crossing of the line,
Behind all is twilight
In front the rosy dawn,
Ahead lies the future
Who has nothing yet to mourn.
Where she has been
There are many mistakes,
Written down and then crossed out
With pencil on a slate.
I look across the radiant valleys
Bathed in the new sunrise,
And see the work of shadows
Though we've only just begun.
Leave your soot and grime and pain,
Bring your promises
Forget your shame,
Run to meet the future.
Hold high the flickering flame,
Now's the time for making good your word
The Angel knows your name.

Elizabeth Maria Rait

A Time Of Grace

> 'And if thou wilt, remember;
> And if thou wilt, forget . . .'
> (Christina Rossetti)

O the dappled days of love years!
The skies so blue above years;
The dancing years - you came into my life.

The early, days of laughter years,
The happy ever after years;
The golden year, when I became your wife!

Came the restless heart years,
The empty, grown apart years,
The wiccan years, that stole my soul from you . . .

And last of all, the true years;
The coming home to you years.
The tender years, of rosemary and rue.

Eileen Pennell

LOOKING FORWARD, LOOKING BACK

It is easier to look back to happy days and lovely places
Than to contemplate the years to come be they short or long
To gaze into the unknown
To cope with galloping future
The accelerating developments that our ageing brains may not grasp
Unless the years behind have been filled with sorrow
And with pain and we still have time to put that right
By putting our hand into the hand of God and accepting His love
To show us the way forward.

Pat Allington Smith

A Millennium Plea

Now that the Dome's been opened,
And the party's all died down.
What of the future for our land,
Where are we heading now?

Let's build a land of freedom,
Where the spirit can soar wild.
Let's make a pledge and mean it,
For each, as yet, unborn child.

A land where gender, creed or race,
Matters not a jot.
A land of opportunity,
And not of 'haves and have nots'.

We're standing at the cross-roads,
Of the future of our kind.
A chance to save this island Earth,
If answers we can find.

So let's all work together,
As we turn another page.
Let this millennium be the one,
That mankind comes of age.

Niall Mclaren

ALTERNATIVE CARGOES
(Inspired By John Masefield's Classic)

Dirty British coaster with a salt-caked smoke-stack,
Chugging up the river to the dock at Tilbury,
With a cargo of wotsits and all sorts of odds-and-sods,
And sailors who try and flog a load of junk to me.

Edith and Catherine, the British railway's ferry boats,
Criss-cross from Gravesend to Tilbury riverside,
With a cargo of workers and shopaholic maniacs,
Checking if the grass is greener on the other side.

Little cabin cruiser, bouncing on the choppy waves,
Driven by a flat-hatted pillock at the wheel,
With a cargo of 'duty frees' he picked up on the continent,
He's hoping that the customs won't put him through the mill.

Great big ocean liner with three majestic funnels,
Heading for the estuary and then off out to sea,
With a cargo of emigrants going to Australia
To start life anew about a million miles away.

Gritty little tug with a whacking great tow-rope,
Pulls along a liner like it doesn't weigh a pound,
With a cargo of stamina to do the job it has to do,
Pulling bigger ships so they don't run aground.

Split-sprit barges with their red sails to the wind,
Splendidly evocative of 'Old Father Thames',
With a cargo of anything that wants taking anywhere,
Sparkling on the water like ruby coloured gems.

See a pensive lad as he sits on the riverbank,
The sights and the sounds in his eyes and his ears,
With a cargo of fantasies, visions, and interest,
And plans for writing poems in his twilight years.

Mick Nash

Ever Hopeful

My own husband fought like many others in the war
He came back looking very weak and very poor,
When I met him at the station
I could not believe the situation
That really this was my husband that I came for.

Now we live beside the sea
Oh! so different for me
In a bungalow where we've lived for fifteen years.
Here I love the sunset that we see from our own windows
But that love is very different
From the way I love my husband
For that love will never, never bring my tears.

If we are both living to the year two thousand and one
We would celebrate our Diamond Wedding, oh what fun!
For our daughter and her husband
Would bring our family together
What a wonderful celebration that would be.

Phyllis M Dunn

THY KINGDOM COME

How can we save a world that is dying,
An Earth in turmoil, its people crying?
Forests destroyed for greedy man's gain,
Buildings eroding through acid rain.
A hole in the ozone, with a planet shrinking,
What on earth are we all thinking?

All manner of diseases have victims taken hold,
We still cannot cure even the simple common cold.
The nation's health has problems so precarious,
To find one a bed, has become so hilarious.
Drugs and crime are at a premium,
The success of the Dome is one in a million.

Flowers of the meadow get more scarce each year,
Buttercups and cowslips gone forever, I fear.
No more do we see all types of butterflies,
The same must be said of the birds of the skies.
Seas are polluted, fish cannot swim,
One must admit things look awfully grim.

Marian Lacy

FRIENDSHIP

Together we traversed highways and byways,
Walked over cliff tops and meadows on many days,
Explored English countryside near and far
Varied by boat, coach, also car.

Viewed Blackpool Illuminations, Amsterdam's night lights,
Fascinated by Quebec and its starlight nights,
Glided along canals in a Venetian gondola,
Pedalled boat on Italian lake, fearful of toppling over.

Captivated viewing Statue Of Liberty, Ellis Island with historic past,
Strolled New York's avenues with memories to last,
Climbed Empire State Building above traffic noise and people,
Panoramic view over skyscraper and steeple.

Visited the Amish sect living within their belief,
Walked among Arlington's dead heroes with thoughts of disbelief,
Helicopter over Niagara, planes flying ocean and seas,
In name of friendship, pleasurable activities such as these.

P Fisk

A New Planet

Up in the skies so far away
we can only dream of the distance -
a star exploded.

Its nuclear fuel exhausted
unstable - unable
to keep within its shell
it expanded
its light increasing
hundred - no - thousandfold.

Were there other worlds near it?
Overwhelmed - now destroyed.
Minute particles
creating a new nebula
that will emit radiation
for thousands of years -

infinitesimal dust motes
swirling in space
looking for company
    gathering
        bonding
            growing
                condensing
to a predestined shape -

until one day there will be
another planet up in the skies
with life-forms like ours?

Maria-Louise Stephens

CENOTAPH

When footsteps stumble
and the body slips
through the cracks
of this broken earth.
Who is there to remember,
to weep
over a grave
that lies unkept?

Let the memories of others
always be true,
and each second of each memory
have been well lived.

But most of all,
no questions and no regrets.

Michael Wilson

LOOKING FORWARD

Don't be someone who forgets
Who you are, where you came from
What is expected of you and where you are
going to.
The distractions along the way
Are many
The help along the way
Is minimal
Everybody wants a part out of you
For themselves
So be careful, be vigilant, step carefully
But step forward.

Zahida Darr

Do We Have To Sign For This

We knocked on the door of the future
Bearing millennium gifts from the past
We thought they'd be happy with what we'd brought
We were wrong, the children were aghast.

We laid out our baubles before them
Our harvest of a thousand wasted years
As we smugly displayed these trinkets
They turned into a million tears.

Each teardrop reflected a small sad face
With cold accusation in its eyes
And as we shrank from their icy stares
We heard a million sighs.

Their tiny voices whispered
'You've sold our future for gain
Leaving drought, disease, famine and war
Greenhouse gases and acid rain.'

We knew then our gifts were unwanted
We knew we were sadly remiss
When one young child from the future asked
'Do we have to sign for this?'

J Brown

Michaelmas Daisy Time

Michaelmas daisies
Poised by the altar:
I am transported
Back to my childhood.

First day at dame-school,
Strange separation -
Mother returning
Heard us reciting.

Poem I learnt then
Still I remember:
Michaelmas daisies
Growing so tall there.

Errors of grammar
Swarmed in this poem,
But sense of wonder
Bid us all follow.

Michaelmas daisies,
Taller than we were,
What did they look at
Over that high wall?

Life would be waiting
With all its marvels
If we kept looking
And really wanted.

September flower,
Time of departures;
Life throws its bridges -
Questions are answered.

Anne Sanderson

REMINISCENCE

Walking the donkeys on the sand
and climbing rocks hand over hand,
fun on the pier, swim in the sea
fairgrounds, rowing, time to feel free,
listen to parents, 'don't be late!'
run out the door, can hardly wait
to take the short cut through the caves,
reach harbour wall to watch the waves,
feel the pebbles under my feet
and buy an ice-cream for a treat.
Hard to believe a war is on
back home, the bombs falling upon
the houses so close to our own
(would worry more if I was grown!)
Anderson shelters at the school
Morrison shelters they were cruel!
torture chambers of three feet high
grills all round, I wanted to fly
out of the house, into the road
watch a 'doodle-bug', will it explode?
Creepy hush it hangs in the air
then dives down, rubble everywhere.
We were lucky, others were not,
time to share with those who'd got
nothing left, goods, homes, all gone,
just the future to build upon.

Ann Odger

THOUGHTS ON THE NEW MILLENNIUM

A Guid New Year we welcome in - hail to the new millennium
As always, fun and cheer and loving celebration.
Yet sometimes leading to sad eventuality and fallen dreams.

What do we see above the parapet of daily life?
The City Yuppies on their greedy, grasping trail
'Gimme, gimme, gimme' - let's go to the very edge and prevail.
Gather ye bonuses while ye may - pay day, pay day, pay day!

And in the Great Chamber by the Thames, the Club debates
The 'grey scrubbers' whipped into a frenzy of contumelious jibes
New this, new that, spin this, spin that - spin the rabbit out of
                                            the eternal hat
Or if other theatricals appeal - attend the Gilbertian frolics of
                                            the Upper Place!

But wait: the wheel looks good, whirling in iridescent joy
Showing us bright horizons and ascendant expectations.
While down at the Dome, the Greenwich Caliban leaves his lair
To flog the wanton imposition of his meretricious wares.

What are we all about? Pilgrims to the retail park?
Past the corner, cardboard box to spend our lives as mere voluptuaries?
Or will we reach out to recognise the gift of giving
To the bleeding poor, to the ever present, ever pleading peripherals?

The future good and vibrant we wish to see
Best of the present and better still to come
New progress made and nation all as one
A wild, triumphant incandescence of terrestrial peace!

Always out there the approaching storm in its barbarity
Threatening to uproot man's humanity and foist on us its
                                        black indexation of despair.
But face the foe, reject the bile of its perversity
And steer our ship to waters of just and consequential gain.

Akran is dead but Aslan lives in full vitality
Symbol of sempiternal good and awesome integrity,
Who challenges man's transcendental need for trekking to the stars!

P G Clarke

BREAKAWAY

Don't do it, don't do it
You will find to your cost
That leaving your home
You will be totally lost.
Don't do it, don't do it,
Whatever you do give up your job
With those elderly two.
Work in an emporium is so hard to find
For someone who is 50,
You are really quite blind.
don't do it, don't do it,
Stay safe at home
Remember, oh remember
You're not young anymore.
I did it, I did it.

Susan Lewis

Exodus

As the nation of shopkeepers
Wakes to the science fiction years
Of wall-to-wall technology -
Where only thoughts are feared.
Brain cells made redundant
Are asset-stripped and then shut down,
Human minds lie stricken, wrecked -
Like ships that ran aground.
Twenty-first century Britain -
Echoes to a purring sound,
Computers now the fat controllers -
In every walk of life they're found.

Computers side-by-side-by-side
Drive the trains they ride,
To work in shops and factories
Stacked so high they touch the sky.
In hospitals they cure,
Filter toxic water pure,
Keeping aeroplanes aloft,
Policing every law.
Engaged in peace and war
Eradicating error - detecting any flaw,
In babies grown outside the womb -
Day trips to the moon,
Transplanted organs harvested -
Freshly farmed from sad baboons,
Maintaining life - assisting death -
In truth they're everywhere,
A computer population boom!
Now no one lives in Britain -
There isn't any room.

Philip Mee

OUT OF THE MIST

'Poor old girl,' they said, ' a bit touched you know.'
Mrs Bolton sat at the window, all and every day.
(it was her life - that is, the rest of it, in every way.)
Open it was, almost to all weather . . .
her face, lined and rutted like a country lane and that together
with screwed-up currant eyes, mouth grinning,
malevolently glad
made her look mad.
Off the pavement and into the road they stepped, rather than pass by.
She mumbled at them and only spoke
to Ellie Watson on her way to school.
'Happy, you must be happy.' Few cackling words, a croak,
Ellie stopped, hop-scotching on one foot.
'I am happy. There's chocolate in my lunch box.'
'Not chocolate, not now.'
'Then how?' A frown, not knowing, not there.
'Next year, on and on, always growing.'
Too much, Ellie shook her head
'Don't know . . .' a gap like eternity, then curious, genuine:
'Will you be dead?'
Mrs Bolton's mouth widened to a smile,
a gentle smile and nothing said.
Too much. Ellie scampered off and soon forgot.
The day stretched covering the afternoon with mist from the river,
down over everything, just grey bands curling, swirling,
Mrs Bolton reached for the future with shaking hands,
fingers scrabbling to tear aside the cloying, the thick and the dumb.
'We are on the king's highway,' said Mrs Bolton with
                                                persistent certainty,
'and all the lights are green.'
She was positive, but so very tired - 'we shall see, we *shall* see.'

Joanna Carr

WHO CARES?

A thousand years have passed by.
Do those celebrating know why?
A thousand years of history in the making,
travel, invention, medicine and research undertaken.

Volcanoes erupt and tornadoes wail
yet a tidal-wave of refuge fills the sea.
Who cares about the fish that lose their tails
when there's 'fish and chips' for our teas.

Who cares about the world which we live in
when we put rockets in the sky
without anyone asking, why?
Doesn't anyone care about living in a refuge bin?

So we raise our glasses to the new millennium
while midnight bells ring it in.
The display of fireworks is impressive
but who cares about the state the world is left in?

Who indeed, cares?

M Lesley Nicholls

2000 - OUR CHILDREN'S LEGACY

2000 could be the start
of triumph or despair,
a time for looking at life's promise
or threats, 2000 depends on
how much you and I care.
2000 could mean the difference between
the beauty of an early dawn,
a fresh new day
or in its place,
the ugly side of nature's face.
It's in our hands,
it is our choice,
shall we ignore the warning signs
destroy the land we all should love,
have no thought for those to come
close our eyes, ignore the voice.
Soft sigh of ocean kissing beach,
autumn's beauty soon to be
snowy white as far as eyes can see.
Jewels beyond value nature shares,
she asks nothing but that we care.

Angela Wakefield

TIME-HONOURED CHRISTENDOM

In the first millennium
The fishpond of the British
Heaved with mating frogs.
Would-be mates came from all directions.
Preoccupied with survival,
They had little but prayer
To combat famine and plague -
No time to develop science or art.

In the second millennium
The tadpoles grew in number.
They crossed Europe to fight crusades.
Their strength developed from within.
The dedicated learned new skills,
Built ships to conquer distant lands.
While they trawled the world for wisdom,
Subject people made them rich.

Will there be a third millennium?
Or will we 'render unto Caesar'
All the good that could spawn
From working on the strength within?
Some first, some tenth or more generations
Of rare and exotic species
Have come from distant lands
To live in our humble fishpond.

If we all love our Gardener, ourselves, our neighbour,
We will honour Christendom in time.

Marion Monahan

A Grandmother's Thoughts For The Next Millennium

Entering this new 2K year of time, we are embracing the system metric,
Whilst the new Greenwich Dome of discovery, is decried by every
                                          media critic.
Our ageing population is faced with a viral influenza epidemic
And the fifty years old health service is now considered geriatric.

Youth in the millennium should pause and free-wheel,
Choosing to travel the many highways that life will reveal.
Music, art and sport, exploration however surreal,
To live peaceful, fulfilled lives through their seven ages deal.

Gene modification, now firmly established here,
For highly dedicated scholars with entrepreneurial flair,
To devise, and not corrupt, the passage of Homo sapient care,
To continue our mysterious march through time, to mankind's
                                                  final tear.

No longer builders of empires; just a small off-shore island,
Linked to a multi-lingual land by rail, air and sea.
Soon to share our currency and perhaps drive on the right hand,
Retaining our ancient language and renowned eccentricity.

What of the silicon chip and old fashioned telecommunication,
Regulating our lives in shopping, banking and fraternisation.
3D interactive TV games, may provide some mental satisfaction,
With modified speech, punctuation and our extensive vocabulary
                                          in total decimation.

And so to families and marriage: in decline we are told.
Who would be a genealogist tracing separated/integrated present
                                                    day fold?

Where, in spite of contraception, passionate lovers new
                                                offspring behold,
And modern values and manners, no longer comply to the
                                                      Christian mould.

When gambling with life in the future, for financial gain, politics
                                                     or spiritual pact,
Remember that what you may plan with Sci-Fi, may be lost to
Sci-Fact.

M McCoy

BRITAIN IN THE THIRD MILLENNIUM

I herald a new millennium for Britain
Which was born of Angles and Celts and Danes
Of Norman and Saxon
And of bloody battles on the plains.

I herald a new millennium for Britain
Which stretched an empire across the world;
Took seas and citadels by storm,
And vast armies and armadas hurled
Across continents; I herald a new millennium
For a Britain which fought dark powers in world wars
And other conflicts before and since
Which saw its sons and daughters leave these shores;

And yet a new millennium for Britain in addition now
Heralds a different outcome: the new world of the third millennium
Will truly test what Britain has become -
Poised is it, to be the hub of new technology,
Of services and of finance and of art?
And will it focus on the energy of youth, of vision
And of spirit at its heart?

My hope is also that my song can sing
That Britain has a role to play
In ridding poverty, hunger and dread evil too
Forever from our valiant history.

Mark Lello

UPSIDE DOWN AND SPINNING AROUND

Dark times fall harshly how dark times are tough,
The days feel so endless and the nights so rough,
All that surrounds you feels cold and bleak,
Streams of tears oh how you may weep.
Illusions and faith expelled from within,
Another world of emotion so tightly locked in,
But do follow your river and do sing your song,
just follow your river for it cannot be wrong.
Run through the fields and breathe the air,
Look up to the skies just gaze just stare,
Feel each day with your heartbeat though it your last,
Steal fond thoughts of the now distant past,
Fly high in the sky like the birds that are free,
See the world in its glory as you dreamed you could see,
For little is greater than your journey through life,
Embrace this truth in times of serenity and times of strife.
Slowly but surely those tears turn to joy,
For upon the horizon your ship is ahoy,
A beautiful chapter may close but you must turn the page,
Love your story and play it proudly upon your stage,
The dark times will fade in time they will go,
Then eternal sunshine can truly glow.

Kurt Perry

WE'RE IN THE YEAR 2000

We're in the year 2000,
What does all this mean.
The fireworks and parties over
And now we start all clean,
Another year has begun alas
And we put another thousand years in the past.

But let us all remember the meaning of it all, a baby born of Mary,
They called Him Christ the Lord.
Christ was born and this is what we know (2000 years ago)
We are all here today to praise Him, this we all do show,
We come to church to pray and show Him that we do care
We rejoice and pray and sing that we do all share.

We're all in this life together, poor or rich or different colour skin,
But Christ is looking after us to shield us from all sin.
The place we live is wonderful, of that there is no doubt,
Countryside - landscape whether it's heavy rain or drought.

Let us all today remember those who have passed throughout this life,
Whether it be a child or a relative, a husband or a wife.
We live this life together, let us do our part
We're in the year 2000, God bless us for a new millennium start.

Amen

N J Ball

MILLENNIUM SHAME

With breaking of new millennium dawn
Heralded forth throughout the world
Nature's songbird chorus sang but sweetly,
Pouring forth without intimidation -
Of degenerate man.

Engaged in hype and ballyhoo of but growing older -
God's ultimate creation in jubilation
Most sadly none the wiser -
Fireworks roar in celebration.

Albeit, in parts there hangs a holocaust silence -
For always aftermath -
and gentle mothers weep
For already the wanton killing goes on!

In our once so peaceful land undivided
A cauldron simmers -
Racial conflict fostered by dogma!
Mythological interpretation indoctrination
For whom with truth can tell?

Politicians in gay revelry
Revered reverence unto glorified prefab -
Self egotism priority
Multi thousand constituents lie in gutter
Millennium knell
Bogus asylum seekers given star treatment
Illegal mongrels likewise fare well -
Curried votes -
Terrorist above defamation
New Labour Gain - Millennium Shame.

Gilbert

THIS IS THE TIME

Drinking, singing, fireworks erupting, in each country the scene
                                                                           was the same,
A new year, a new millennium, a new birth, a new death,
So much hope, so much pessimism,
Moving forward not forgetting but instead learning,
Strong emotions and reflections start the year,
Well I had a moment so I thought I would let you know.

From hunting and gathering to internet shopping,
Would you believe a man on the moon, women in work,
A need for fast cars or television dependence,
Records to CDs, mini skirts or flares,
Past visions are now accepted realities,
But still more is wanted and there is much more to give,
However people over money and love over hate
Is not always the philosophy of which life is lived,
Well I had a moment so I thought I would let you know.

If I was to confess for one hope for the future,
it would involve education of the pain caused by wars
And of the much needed development in curing diseases,
As then we could recognise what is important,
Eliminating the ignorance that hurts so many,
Decreasing the level of poverty, homelessness and abuse,
Perhaps even raising a society that is defined as one,
Well I had a moment so I thought I would let you know.

Yes a big dream and yes a big hope,
But determination, recognition and awareness could witness a change,
That's my hope,
Well I never knew you but I think of you,
What would you make of the millennium age generation of your family!

Sarah Payne

WESSEX

Sometimes it seems
Like yesterday's ghost
Haunts the wedding today,
As Edward's bride
The nation's pride
Makes a promise to obey;
As she walks the aisle
With a shy little smile
We remember that other young bride
Her father's pride
The nation all at her feet,
She gave him her heart
But soon they were apart
And the young bride felt defeat;
So she haunts them today
To remember the way
She loved and she lost
And all that it cost
How soon she was gone
That lovely young swan
The cygnets echo her still,
And shy Di's face
Is framed in her Will;
But let us still bless
Wessex's fine young countess!

Margaret Boles

AT THE EVENTIDE HOME, SCALLOWAY

Old Peter sits in the window seat
And watches the boats in the bay.
He nods and smiles and dozes a bit
And hasn't a lot to say;
Perhaps because he's remembering
Other ships and other sails,
And storms and wrecks and young men's deeds
That are now just old men's tales.
If I had the gift of artistry
What a picture that would be!
The face, the smile, the favourite pipe,
And the rug about the knee.

Stella Shepherd

Britannia Weeps

So precious is the untamed sea,
protector of these shores
Caress and rage the tyrants cage
Freedom always reigns.

On shifting sands she makes her stance
For who's the monarch now,
Who holds the key, the crown, the throne?
Traitors in a stranger's home.

Europe's ways conflicting days
For men with arms and scheming plans
The beast is on the move.

Britannia sleeps as treason seeps underneath the door
Her borders bare great men stare
Her unity no more.

Maxwell Anderson

To Be Or Not To Be!

In the beginning there was God –
Who to cast out darkness, made light.
Earth, sky and sea became matter –
Stars, planets and moons added wholeness.
Then God designed man by His powerful might,
To make, mar or flatter –
The scheme, the beauty.

Each century, generation and decade,
Has added, yet subtracted
Something from that beauty.

Throughout the ages, technology has evolved
From the simple to the fantastic.
Yet is a table less important than a car?
Now at present.

A radio less in design or thought than a rocket?
Really – to what purpose the latter?

The modern mind of man can go far –
Producing the unknown as yet.
But will he make good use of this
Constant increase of knowledge?
In this I fear will be his
Downfall and destruction.

Take great care mankind, not to be no more:
To be extinct will be meaningless.
Too clever – yet not clever enough –
To eliminate self-destruction.
In the end there is God.

Maureen Astley-Mullen

MOVING ON

Peaked waves relentlessly cut the stillness
in nature's untamed beauty over the river.
The distant brightness confused whether to illuminate
or to remain darkened.
Fresh salt air triggers reflection, inspiration and
renewed hope for this new millennium.

For the first time in years, I feel in harmony with the elements.
At peace with the past, at one with the future - focused once again.
A time to make adjustments and improvements.
Simple joys of millennial proportions
as its first dawn approaches to rejuvenate and invigorate.

Distant mountains separate yet also bind the young sky
with the quiet land, giving clues to ancient times.
They have no eyes, but have seen it all.
Stars above disappearing from view by life-giving rays spreading -
I think of my children.
They promise so much as time stands still during this moment . . .

Hopes and dreams focused as sharp as the air I breathe
and as vivid as the colours I see around me.
Heady, intoxicating euphoria drowns my mind.
Deep breaths spread the pleasure to every point,
reviving me to surrounding forces and balance within.

Each thought expressed now reminds me of life's ups and downs,
family, friends of old and of friends as yet unknown.
The perfect silence only broken by a seagull's laughing taunts.
White clouds bubble up slowly from nowhere,
their silvered edges hypnotise me at their stunning effect.
Three hours standing still, pass as three minutes.
Lost to time and the future.

Paul R Giannandrea

A Perfect World

If fairy tales could come to life
with end to war and no more strife
from Brussels there'd be no EU
sitting there telling us what to do.
About why cucumbers should all be straight
And we must have the Euro before it's too late.
If trains would always run to time
even if there were leaves on the line.
No rude graffiti on the wall
and could there be no more football?
No baseball hats and 'bovver boots'
and nobody to give two hoots
if Arsenal won or lost the game
and whether the Ashes remain the same.
Families would learn to talk again
not get square eyes and dormant brain.
Children would learn to play together
grown-ups would only discuss the weather
not who was who and what was what
and will Camilla be queen or not!
My fairy tales would all come true
if the world could only start from new
and remember where we all went wrong
and learn afresh as we go along.

Kath Barber

2000

At times when I think of the present date
I wonder what occurrences I await,
In the future, seems far away now,
But occasionally I wonder how
Ordinary tasks shall be accomplished
By robots maybe, although I wish:
As a new millennium is upon us
We should resolve to treat the world around us
With loving care and more respect,
Otherwise usual life aspects
Will pollute and destroy Mother Nature,
Or perhaps we can learn to be more mature,
Have inventors produce an electrical car,
Instead of wearing gas masks due to exhaust fumes,
I would rather by far!
We can only hope people will be more thoughtful,
Not let species become extinct and not be overpowerful.
The new millennium is a new beginning.
Let's start improving, now, in the year 2000.

Jessica Preston

THIRD MILLENNIUM

Something to celebrate, at last!
End of life on the planet,
We call it something else;
'The Millennium!'
What arrogance,
As if our shorter breaths
Bear no conclusion.
No. We're here to go,
And go soon,
And that,
just when love
Had begun to appear,
If only in pockets.

Alfred Warren

Looking Back

Twilight descends and the light of day
Is obscured by mist, darkness and cold.
Along comes an ashen-faced figure,
I saw him, he looked bent, frail and old.

Black-mittened hand gripped a handlebar
Of a bike, too big for his frame;
He balanced a pole precariously,
A cloth cap, shielding him from the rain.

Children now safely home from their schools,
Tho' in those days so little to fear,
Breadwinners scurrying home from their work,
Noisy boots on the pavement you'd hear.

Gathering shadows, ghostly and dark
Banished fragmented light from the day;
As our friend trudged on with his burden,
His cold breath, seen like steam, on the way.

You may know of whom I describe here.
If you're roughly the same age as me,
He's the old lamplighter of long ago,
Who gave such joy, for us all to see!

I was young then, and watched from the parlour,
As he lifted the long pole up high,
Carefully lighting all of the lamps
So the angels could see from the sky.

Life in those days was terribly hard,
To our hearts the light brought a warm glow;
The lamplighter - well, he was pure magic,
I was there, and it really was so!

Robina Karasek

My Memories

When I'm sitting all alone and everything is still
I start to remember things in my life and my eyes begin to fill,
I think of my family both present and past
and think of the good times, why couldn't they last.

I remember my parents, my brothers as well
who suddenly left me before I could tell
how much I loved them and wish they were here,
but I know in my heart they will always be near.

The memories I have I will keep till I die,
of the days that I laughed and the days that I cried,
I think of the people I've loved and adored
And those who I've hated and been thoroughly bored.

But the past has gone and the future's ahead
memories to come and some that I dread,
but life must go on for all that it's worth,
I'm glad I have memories of my life here on earth.

Alan Rogers

THE PITS

The sun was shining another glorious day.
Then Da shouts 'Come on son, let's be on our way.'
Down the pit where the sun never shines
Who the hell wants to work down the mines,
A mile deep, two miles wide.
The Earth opened up, the men went inside
Into her belly to dig for coal
A living to earn from a ruddy great hole.
The siren went off, for some too late,
Women and children at the top, stand and wait,
Waiting for some will be in vain,
But they go down again, they must be insane.
Here in Yorkshire, there's now't else to be,
But a miner puts food on his table you see,
The men die young,
The women, lonely and old
They've sold their lives to the damned black gold.

Janet Follett

Goodbye To The Twentieth Century

I've lived with my time.
I was sad to see last year end it.
It wasn't all sublime,
But I'm ready to defend it.

We're criticised for wars
And frightening inventions,
But we fought for a Cause
And had some good intentions.
Don't we get some applause
For starting Old Age Pensions?

Famines and plagues held sway
And tribal wars were fought
Aeons before our day;
But no one had ever thought
Of holidays with pay.
- Or even felt they ought.

Romans had war-machines
But none to wash their jeans;
Grecians had fine aesthetics,
But we have anaesthetics.
Red Indians had endurance,
But never health insurance.

The best comes at the end:
We thought of the weekend!
Others could hail New Year,
Watching our century go,
But I gave ours a cheer
And called 'Toro Bravo!'

Susan Glyn

THE MILLENNIUM AT LAST

When I was young and starting school at about
The age of four
In the year of '32; our rent was 13 bob a week
]And we were very poor.
We lived in a terraced house three stories high,
The front door opened onto the street,
With a backyard, four-walled and paved with
Hard blue diamond bricks, quite neat.
An outside loo and coal house with tar paper roof
My dad had made.
Way back then I thought of now, the last year of an age
And would I make the grade.
Well . . . here I am, I'm 71; I guess I have it all,
A lovely home with all mod-cons
And hi-tech from wall to wall, two TVs, hi-fi,
Computer, fax/phone and AOL.dot.com,
Washing machine and fridge-freezer, microwave,
A whirlpool bath and a car that's fast.
We've walkmans and CD players to fix upon
Your belt and a mobile phone; I've made it,
The millennium at last . . .

Kenneth Jackson

Untitled

Lonely nights in a big city shroud,
sitting at an empty table,
empty smiles as I look around.
I see the clock on the wall as its second hand ticks
and the hour hand goes round.
you sit and watch your day of the year again come around.
A new year, new town, new number,
if six was nine it's most certainly now.

The city moans once again,
the end of the day, the sun goes down
and the city's glow lights the sky red.
We wait for another day to begin.
In the night the city harbours her battle of respect and sin.
Red sky,
red lights,
Soho girls on the street work the night,
quick talk, fast walk.

The smell of the street.
Rubbish in a sewer reeks and the homeless beg on the passers-by,
for money to buy a cup of tea and food to eat,
they're half-cut , staggering and can hardly speak.

Slowly cruising passing cars
hiding behind panel security.
Washed in the night's street for what pleasure they seek
on these city streets.
Unwashed by the light of day,
the city's heart beats night and day.
Tick-tock, tick-tock, heart beats, city streets.
Tick-tock, ageless clock, tick stop.

Terry Williams

WALKING ON THE RIGHT SIDE

We walk upon this land so green
with dust around our heels,
we seldom think what we have done
why crops won't grow in the fields.
Government coats breed on the land,
they inform us it will make life better,
what is the point of giving us hope
when we all know it won't get better.
The soil is drained of life itself,
Weather-beaten and eaten from within,
the crust of Earth is dying now,
that is a global, nationwide sin.

Les J Croft

POWER TO A NINETY YEAR OLD

'I bathed in the twilight,'
She smiled, 'that wild night.'
Whilst I recalled the sudden blight
Blank nothing - eclipse of doom.
Our mole-like pawing room to room,
Bumping walls, loss of sight.

'I dried my hair by bright fire light,'
She continued, 'that wild night.'
Whilst we'd shivered and cowered
Under a chastising shower,
Candled back to primitive power.
The boiler still, no radio, nor TV.
Disquiet in our chilled-off company.

'I made toast and tea, the paraffin burned,'
Magic lanterns of memories returned.
'I was back at the farm, you know,
The horses, hens, water from the well,
Hard work, no harm to tell.
Of course, it's long ago.
How did you get on that stormy night?'

The old clock chimed, went on ticking,
In time and tune with her click, click knitting . . .

Meg Pybus

Millennium's Mirth

No future is plain to see,
not even where we'd like to be.
Conflicts that continue through the years,
Will keep bringing home our constant fears.
Then this, the future must not be,
So deaths of the past please let us see.
That no more wars will reign upon this earth,
So we can at least enjoy our new millennium's mirth.
throw away the evil guns that harm,
Talk instead worlds of peace that charm.
This then is the way we must surely entreat,
For the world to be forever at our feet.

R F Short

FUTURE HOPES

We all need a little magic in our lives to overcome so much unwelcome
intrusion.
Although we know to exist in a world of fantasy would be merely
an illusion.
And yet, we must choose somewhere between what is becoming
commercial and aggressive,
Where sentiment and affection are becoming second place and other
feelings are obsessive.
If we looked around we see many of the young are setting an
example in the race,
And although some are justifiably blamed for much of the mayhem,
they will set the pace.
They are the ones who can decide on their future world to enhance
or destroy.
It needs to be brought home to them, that they have a duty, every
girl and boy.
Every act of vandalism or destruction puts the clock back a
little more,
So that the legacy that they should be proud of, to this they
close the door.
We are seeing almost daily the ones who've taken advantage of
technology available to everyone,
Yet there are those who have no constructive ambition and so
much time has gone.
Despite this we must be optimistic, that there are more who care
and have respect.
And we all must hope the balance does not get out of hand, it's not
too much to expect.

Reg Morris

What Have We Done

There is a light that goes out in all of us
like the setting of the sun,
When your time has come upon this Earth
who will ask what you have done.

Will it be that you have helped to conceive
the fruits of God's fair land,
Or did you scheme and cheat your way
or just grovel in the sand.

The second millennium is now at hand
let us look at the world as a whole,
With poverty, war and starvation
it's about time we looked into our soul.

Is this how God had intended
are we to strip fellow man of his worth,
Robbing our planet of its resources
until there is nothing left of our Earth.

The sand timer is running
do we just take for your pleasure or mine,
Or will it be when the last grain has fallen
you meant nothing in Earth's passage of time.

The world's supermarket is running empty
there are no more deliveries to be made,
It is time for us to stop shopping
before our life is permanently in the shade.

John Hewins

If Only Now We Find The Way To Love!

While nations dream of glory and of might
We see the ghosts of marching men at night,
Like roses full of promise from the bud
That quickly died and sank beneath the mud.

While power gave commands that some must die
And man believed the voice that told a lie,
The aged heart cried out in dreams once more
And ghostly forms lay still upon the shore.

While freedom was a future offered men
And laughter faded from the Highland Glen,
There flowed sad tears in painful disbelief
From aged hearts of nations in their grief.

While honour touched the vein of vanity
The mind was closed to all reality,
So then the face revealed its final pain
On blood-red earth where beauty once had lain.

While people saw their dreams in fast decay
And blooms of youth and love had slipped away,
The age heart was kneeling down in prayer
And weeping broke the silence everywhere.

While seasons change and I look back in time
I praise the bells of harmony that chime,
Within the hearts of colour, creed and race
And all the lands that offer friendly grace.

While friendship moves the world to joyful peace
True happiness shall wear her Golden Fleece,
And souls shall fly to Heaven like a dove,
If only now we find the way to love!

Peter James O'Rourke

Distant Times

A long time ago in a far distance past,
I once knew happiness when we all played together and laughed
    from day to day.
Occasional trips to the park.
Summers seemed endless, yet school still a chore,
Those idle days of yesteryear I long for once more.
Races, tig, stuck-in-the-mud, kick the can and much more,
Just a fading memory now of happy times gone by.
The feelings of warmth, friendship and happiness still linger on.
Now like those summers, friends have moved on to different
    destinations, families new.
In these troubled modern times, I wonder what has become
    of you, childhood innocence too.

Foy Kennedy

THE FUTURE

Dreams and hopes, laughter and tears
Surrounded by millennium fears.
Will the bug disrupt the earth,
Filling us with heartache and mirth.
Or will our new century dawn
In a world that's kind and warm.
Where people love instead of hate
Where wars do not decide our fate.
Will the Lord from glory come,
Deciding that his work is done.
Who knows what the year two thousand will bring,
Will all nations turn away from sin.
Let's drink to a future where people care,
A land of plenty we all can share.
Holding hands together in love,
As first was planned by God above.

Stella Van Onselen

All It Takes

Coolness dabbed me crown, as I lumber -
swung from the sliding door.
A dangle of signs on bended knees
pitched in a flummox of either/or.

When that was then, it looked so real,
I thought, emerging from a trim. It's odd
those angles, curves and corners stayed
in place right through the interim.

I stopped upon a cornerstone. Each new sight
marked another kingdom to the fore.
'Hurry on,' came a voice behind. 'No time to stare
(or comb your hair); get back in line, you hear?'

And in those dragon times, when summer's face
turned fiery on a curling hill, a life ago
already was a life away - mulled and whirled;
turned in the glow of the lightening day.

And with unblinking eyes, even as steam
turned sinews by the park. Like wandering
in a memory-lot: too late? too soon? It comes
to heart that all it takes is all we've got.

Lionel Stanbrook

Looking Forward

Friday evening arrives
To an audible sigh
From every corner.

The weekend is here
With the promise
of rest, or a change.

Hurrah! Shout the kids.
No school for two days.
What shall we do?

Are we going away?
Or going out to play?
Or is it computer games?

While mother sighs
For the holidays she's due:
Please! I must get away.

She pleads a trip
When Dad gets home.
He listens with half an ear.

Not this week, he says.
I've other plans.
There's lots of jobs to do.

Terry Daley

NEW FOR OLD

As each year goes another comes
Again and again and then,
Every 1,000 years a new millennium.
So as we celebrated one and all
Around the world each nation called
For peace and joy good will to all men
In the ideal world but when?
No more wars, no more sorrow
Each is waiting for a better tomorrow.
Each has our own memories through our lives
Some bad, some good, how hard some tried.
Natural disasters man-made catastrophes
Science and nature go hand in hand
A trip to unknown worlds in the sky.
Modern technology can now reveal
Secrets of the universe are secrets no more.
The marvellous achievements give us more leisure
Time to enjoy, oh what a pleasure
Through the years our childhood days
Optimism and pessimism some of each in us all
Pick ourselves up for a new start when we fall.
A home is the most wonderful place to be
For the quality of life for you and me
This does not change with passing time
We are caretakers for future generations
All the things and places we have
So our contribution to this cause will be
New for old for all to see.

M Baker

THE NEXT MILLENNIUM

In the next Millennium
Will we see
Holidays to the moon
Or down in the depths of the sea?

Will we go to school
Or maybe use a laptop
Or have a robot teacher
That never tells you off?

Will we wear our normal clothes
Or a special spacesuit?
Will we eat cyber food
Or genetically modified fruit?

Will people visit museums
To look at an ancient corn-on-the-cob
And wonder what a book was
And why we bothered to get a job?

Maybe it will all go wrong,
And the planets will line up,
And there'll be tidal waves and hurricanes,
And that will be the end of us!

Rachel Greener (11)

The British Ride

Our polyglot, island race,
Proud conquerors once of land and sea,
Today some say we've lost
Our real identity.

We kid ourselves when quickening pace
That flags of political correctness
And surfing the net,
Will give us what
We need to get,
A twenty-first century ride
To a sense of non-national pride.

Inventors still invent,
And art is unmade beds,
Our money ebbs and flows,
But these do not prevent
The quintessential Britishness
From breaking out and howling,
'No! We will never surrender
Our eccentricities.'
And that's the way true Britons go,
Giving, taking and keeping.

Stephanie Mottram

OUR FUTURE?

The third millennium's here to stay
(Nostradamus didn't get his way)
I fear for what our future holds,
The world's in a mess, we don't need to be told.
We've helped destroy the ozone layer
So global warming now we fear.
Britons, once recognised by face,
Have become a multi-national race.
Black and white, even yellow,
All mixed up, joined together.
The family unit is no more,
Though babies still are born galore.
Law and order have broken down,
Criminals hold sway in every town.
The country's bankrupt, could it be
Too much Social Security?
The Government's finally met its fate,
We're now part of the European State.
Royalty has had its day,
Just told to go, they had no say.
The future's held in all our hands,
So let us try and save this land,
Pray that God will help us be
A nation, peaceful, in unity, free,
Part of a Universal Plan
To survive to the next millennium.

Eileen Ayres

CHILDREN AT WAR

Do you remember, little brother,
The old tin tub that hung on a hook in the yard,
Friday nights full of dread, blackout curtains pulled tight,
Smoky lamp that scattered the dark?

You were the smallest and shed the least dirt,
So you were first in the queue
For ritual immersion, a slip'ry pink squirm
That emerged baptised, squeaky new.

On to the fire more buckets of warm,
The next shouted into the bath,
Much crying and wailing, 'There's soap in my eye.'
While I toasted bread on the hearth.

When we all had been washed and shampooed and dried,
Put in freshly baked linen and parked in a line,
With soft Celtic cursing, scummy water tipped out
To nourish the garden outside.

Then we'd sit down with scissors and pieces of string,
To contribute to Hitler's downfall,
The 'News Of The World' neatly cut six by six
To hang from a nail in the wall.

Upstairs with a candle to soften the night,
Hurl into the goose-feather bed,
Listen to miners return from their shift,
Ebon faced, rheumy eyes rimmed with red.

In your two-bathroomed house, little brother you live,
Velvet windows and heavy oak door,
Neatly pressed lawns lead down to the pool,
But the children of war are still here.

Elisabeth Ware

GREETINGS

In the present,
is the future echoed back,
as if tomorrow's present,
cast like a shadow into our present,
our present being the future's yesterday cast like a shadow
on itself.
For we being shadows of ourselves cast from the future,
into our own past,
And the whole world and all its players present, merely
cast shadows of the future.

And in the future,
the whole world's stage and all its actors,
their shadows cast into their own past,
and wherein these haunting shadows,
we may in the present sense as if the future was staring
back at us.

So that the whole round of the world,
of the fabric of all things and of the Earth,
and all its people cast into its own past,
that in the present we may hear echoes from the future,
So that one day we may wave to ourselves,
and see in the future,
people waving back,
and send each other greeting cards.

Anthony Maccini

You Do Not See Yourself As You Are

Janus looks at his reflected self
in B. J. Jones' polished window.
It is not him, for he feels young.
The image that stares back
is old and crumpled.

Like a balancing toy clown
he wobbles back into December,
the rush to spend, spend, spend.
To defeat the dark days,
and long black nights.

He can't find the now,
the drifts of lighter afternoons,
snowdrop explosions, buds on branches,
the silent growth towards
the fanfare of spring.

Backwards and forwards time tumbles
each month catches his breath
and is blown away, as the calendar turns.
He is caught again
on the cusp of old and new.

Sue Moules

MILLENNIUM

The old century with vibrant colour fades,
The piper brings an awakening dawn
Of millennium's silver schemes.
Hills are remembered - though distant;
Food tastes familiar to the palate.
Old friends are gone - or far away
A robotic future awaits.
Heaven still sends its Guardian Angels.

Irene Patricia Kelly

SACRED HORSE'S GHOST

Sacred Horse's ghost.
Listens to the last post.
From the Pony Soldiers' fort.
They've stolen his land
And scattered his band.
They've slipped through his fingers like sand.
They've killed the buffalo,
Brought bigotry and dread,
Carnage and hunger,
Flight and fear, they've stolen his bread.
Forced reservations, white man's ways.
Gone are the happy, carefree, hunting days.
Trading with the Pawnee.
War'ing with the Sioux.
I wear my weather dancer's shirt
After I saw it in a dream.
I hold my 'sun dance' doll
With its power to grant revenge.
The buffalo, our buffalo are gone
And the red hunter must die of hunger.
Hands painted on my chest
Show I have killed an enemy
In hand-to-hand combat.
But now the white eyes, hunt me with cannon
And we trek through the snow to escape.
But there is no escape.
We are to be no more.
Just a distant memory
As the land is taken from us
And changed forever more.

Paul Belshaw

SECOND CHANCE

As man goes staggering forth from New Year fling,
Does he deserve you, oh Millennium Spring?
You, fresh and faithful with your April gloss,
Him, stale and faithless with his winter dross.

Come darling buds proclaim a thousand Springs,
Come flowers blossom as the robin sings,
And as another hopeful dawn begins,
Go Mammon and repent a thousand sins.

Peter Davies

HOMELESS

Forgive me Lord for what I've done, I passed her in the street
She called me more than once, I choose to take interest in my feet
When looking back I saw her face, so young and yet so old
The streets have not been kind to her, dark eyes see only cold.

A little change I could have spared, a hot meal I could provide
I chose to walk away from her, to walk away and hide
Pretty once she might have been, replaced by a hardened life
No fixed abode, no place called home, a daily dose of strife.

I'm sorry for the life she leads, the way that she must feel
The shop doorway, cardboard box, and her food she has to steal
As well as her there's many more, what a life they have to live
Next time like me when walking past, remember try to give.

Let's make their lives a little easier, better for them to bear
Not leave the world a darkened place, and for them so unfair
They bring it upon themselves I know that we all say
Together let's understand and lighten up their darkest day.

Caryne Crane

THERE WAS A TIME . . .

There was a time
a past reflection,
when I believed in love.

Nothing could fail
no fear of rejection,
she was pure as a dove.

But alas I was wrong
the birds stopped their song,
and beauty drifted away.

My soul got burnt
a lesson learnt,
she crushed my heart like clay.

Now there's people I meet
and acknowledge a wink,
connect with their internal despair.

They've had their hearts broke
treated like a joke,
love became lost in the air.

Alan J Hedgecock

Past, Present And Future

When we were young, we lived in the present,
with a daily routine:
meal times, play, school and sleep.
Little did we worry, though a war
was raging both abroad and nearer home.
It even claimed my Father, when I was only three.
Security was all around us -
Mother, pets, toys and home.

When we were grown and done with studying,
those childhood memories faded,
as work, love, home-making intervened
and became the new present time.
We planned, made new acquaintances,
and dreamed about a future free from cares.

When we raised our children, we looked back
on our own childish games and fantasies,
to pass tradition on to a new generation.
Older and wiser now,
we look both past and forwards,
fondly recalling precious youth and growth.

Now we think towards the future
with hope, or maybe hidden fear, inside.
Our strength may be diminished, but
our experiences all the more in number.

We can be certain of the past – it happened.
We can be sure about the present; we are in it.
We can only hope and pray for days to come,
and put our future in the hand of God.

J M Gardener

A Double Edged Sword -
In The Hands Of Time

We rush forever onwards
In a race against the time
Though we have travelled far
Along, this winding meridian line

This century has flourished with inventions
In this powerful jet-engined age
The elegant supersonic Concorde
Moon rockets and the satellite space craze

With the wheel, came motor vehicles
So we needed motorway linked roads
Stream brought us trains and rail tracks
Soon deadly pollutions were exposed

Electricity produced by nuclear power stations
Blasting out yet more harmful fumes
TV's, videos, radios and piped music
Gadgets live in our homes in every room

Medical science has advanced
Cloning, far beyond our remotest dream
Delicate and refined transplant surgery
Disease cures, and laser's powerful beam

Telephones have now become mobile
Chips, Internet and computers rule our world
Will there still be a need for people
As the time-path uncurls

Countries still wage, war after war
The destruction and killing never stops
How far down this road must we travel
Before we stop and count the cost.

Christina B Cox

Forty Years Ago I Was Seven

Every weekend with my parents,
We went to Laneham, caravaning and boating
Where we met many people and friends were made.
Sometimes I've been with them again at home.
We are transported then, back in time to Laneham days.
Laughter is heard everywhere!
We enjoyed those weekends, up to me being seventeen years old
My parents at home were visited by all kinds of people
From the Laneham days.
Their lives had changed just like them.
Laneham kept their memories young and alive,
Which all had shared.
Forty years ago, when I was seven!

Michèle Umpleby

THE MARCH OF TIME

I remember serving as a Wren,
chez Fleet Air Arm there strove I
in my small way, helping fighting men
who flew engines in the sky;
But defying war soared high morale;
hectic times were had by all,
tangoing past the ferocious snarl
of Luftwaffe's lethal brawl;
and, on Sundays, Wrens went on parade,
such distinctive, rousing sight,
secondary to thrills of flight.
An ex-Wren and elderly has-been,
I hear the spirited music play,
fine attribute of adept Marine;
I'm revelling in that sound today.
Now the bleak horizon looms ahead;
Shall the swelling drum-beats blend,
those that glorify, extol the dead
timelessly, world without end?
Convoluted principles divide
peacemaker from war agent,
mundanity turns robot world-wide.
Did tune fade where marchers went,
dignified though vivid with remorse
that common man sink so low,
taking conflict as matter of course?
Shall we dreamers live to know?

Ruth Daviat

THE THIRD MILLENNIUM RACE

The double digit day has gone.
I see no sign that things went wrong.
The planes still flying in the sky
By dint of use of magic eye.
The blind will see in similar way.
With ray and chips until the day,
That genes are changed from nature's dread.
By men who with the gods do tread.
All humankind
From foot to mind
Now formed by man
With long life span.
Three hundred years of life on earth,
Where imperfections are a dearth.
Where choice and vision rule supreme
And all else solved by time machine.
Computers have begun to think
The future's found the missing link
When silicon placed beneath your skin
Make robots now your kith and kin.
The British race
That once ruled proud
Got lost in space
Amongst the crowd.

Robert Lumley

QUESTIONS FOR THE LONDON EYE

London Eye what will you see when the dawn of the new millennium
becomes warmed by our tireless sun
and the Dome has swapped its propagandist stalls and stages
for the thrill machines designed to part the masses from their money?
Will you see a country that discovers, just in time
The emptiness of soul that relentless pursuit of wealth and power
brings to the collective consciousness of the people
to become embedded in the blueprint of future generations?
And as the waxing and waning moon continues its unhurried path
Will those who proclaim and pronounce on God's behalf
themselves begin to see the spiritual needs of the people laid bare,
and start the gradual thawing of their hearts
In advance of global warming?
Ambitious hopes on the crest of the new millennium wave!
Of little matter to those who watched the fireworks from their concrete
beds or the river of fire through a heroin haze.
But without ambition and hope expressed
The case for the world is lost before the trial commenced.

So a toast to all who bequeathed us their genes
and our privileged place in the world,
who built us our monuments and made all our wars.
Will the London Eye look proudly upon the lessons we learned from
this past?
or shed its tears for a people, so blind,
that they could not see the wonderful, wonderful world this could be?

Sandra Game

3rd Millennium - The Outcome

For centuries we've been a United Kingdom, Britain,
Four countries together as one, but will it so remain
To survive a third millennium; will what was once Great
Become fragmented, no longer United, but separate,
For all the progress that man, with science has made,
The inborn sense of survival, the clannishness, still bades
Us deep down, to embrace that for which our ancestors fought,
The dawn of the third millennium has brought
This disintegration closer; Scotland, political revolution,
Wales will be next in the clamour for devolution,
And Ireland, with its religious fissure,
How much more, can, or will its citizens endure?
And what of England? Now a melting pot of cultures,
Her identity slowly devoured, yet stoically clinging, as vultures
To a carcass, to traditions of old, whilst marching on,
Proud; by the fourth millennium will Great Britain be gone.

C Carey Jones

OUR TIME

So much has happened, where do we start?
Who would have known you could have a new heart.
Remedies, potions and cures for most ills,
Can you really believe our food will be pills?
A trip to the moon for the man on the street,
Will we be a part of this amazing feat?
Great men have achieved many wondrous things
But can't prevent wars and the heartache this brings.
When will we learn to live in peace,
To end all bloodshed and let the killing cease?
Man must look forward and learn from these horrors
With faith, then rebuilding towards our future tomorrow.

Olive Noad

Two Thousand Years

'The Millennium's coming,' they said, 'What fun!
Let's gather round and plan;
What can we do to celebrate, what lavish our money on?'
So sixty sat thinking grandiose thoughts, really wracking their brains
For something to please folk throughout all the realm;
And give them Parliamentary gains.
'Sorry, what's that you ask?' said one. 'Why celebrate at all?
Isn't it two thousand years of something, or since?'
'I don't know; but the Third Millennium will be here soon,
Look at the calendar there on the wall.
Oh, I see what you mean, sorry, the arithmetic's mine,
Another twelve months before the Second one's gone!
But it's two thousand years, of something, or since; never mind,
Let's party, it'll do us all good, we've had such a terrible time.'

The Millennium's almost here.
'What's that mean?'
Asks the starving African child,
With ribs you could play a tune on
And a belly swollen with pain.
'Don't know,' says his Indian cousin,
Carefully picking her way
Through the stinking filth of a Bombay slum,
To the hovel that is her home.

The Millennium's almost here. My God! Have we nothing better to do
Than spend billions on meaningless trinkets and domes?
Is this how to 'celebrate', using brain-power and cash?
Have the two thousand years been nothing to us but columns of numbers of days?

When our days are all up, what will we say,
When we're asked to account for our time.

Arthur W Gilliland

MILLENNIUM HOPE

What can the new millennium bring
To put the world to rights.
Bring back the national service
For those who like street-fights.
Instead of sending men into space,
Spend the money and help to give
Food for the hungry, help for the poor
And the homeless a place to live.
Help all the children of the world
To live a life without fears
So they can learn to laugh and play
And not see war and tears
If we can all just take the time
To help each other out.
The world would be a better place
Of that I have no doubt.

D Hayter

Untitled . . .

The year of Our Lord, is three thousand and ten
I have never seen the sea, a duck or a hen.
I have never seen blue sky, I've never seen rain
I have no feelings, for pleasure or pain.

No money to spend nowhere to go
To lie in the grass, play with you in the snow
There's no day or real night, artificial that's me
I have no friends or family for tea.

You wonder how I know of the things that you do
How you smiled when you're happy or cried when you're blue.
I'm a computer from future, your destiny, your will
I've stored all your memories, wrote on parchment with quill.

Pictures I have of the stories you tell
But the things I can't store are a touch or a smell
Fresh bread that's being baked or flowers that bloom
The fragrance of pine the scent in a room.

High-tech killed this planet there's no one left here
There's a vortex, a vacuum, no pubs and no beer.
It was hate killed the planet with chemicals and greed
Nothing will grow now, no love and no seed.

I'm the only survivor, I'm the only one here
It's like starting again, will man reappear.
I'm your destiny, your future, will you listen to me
You'll destroy your nice planet, just wait and see.

Numero Uno 99

Charles Wayne Leadbeater

HISTORY TOMORROW

Irish peace and farewell House of Lords,
First fruits of the Pan-European state.
So, see you around Britain
Look after yourself
We'll have a drink sometime.
Cheerio, as I wave you, goodbye.
And it wasn't that they opposed the Ecu
They just liked Stirling strung to Wall Street.
And it wasn't that they opposed federalisation
They just liked policy conceived in boardrooms
So , see you around Britain
Watch how you go
We must do lunch sometime
Cheerio, as I wave you, goodbye.
So, no more, I am British
Then, no more, I am European
But high held heads and hand on heart
I am Human.
So, see you around Britain
Make sure your coat's done up
It's a windy history out there.
Cheerio,
        as I wave you,
                goodbye.

Cardinal Cox

Millennium Dreams

What does it mean to you
This new millennium?
What are your hopes and dreams
In all the years to come?

Does it mean a new beginning,
Forget about the past?
Did you celebrate it quietly,
Or did you have a blast?

Did you make some resolution
Things you must and mustn't do?
Or do you think this year
Your dreams just might come true?

Well whatever you are wishing
Throughout the coming years
Let's raise a glass to everyone
Good luck to all and cheers.

Trisha Buchanan

THROUGH THE EYES OF LOVE

I'm bored Nan - are you? Oh no, not me
I'm watching a woodpecker in that tree
I'm listening to the humming of a bumble bee
Making honey for someone's tea.
Why don't you come and sit with me
There's plenty more for us to see.

A Jenny wren with his tail up high,
Shapes of clouds that form in the sky
The drone of a plane passing by -
The long slender wings of a dragonfly.
A proud little robin with a red breast
Somewhere close she has a nest
Her babies first flight will be put to the test
Slowly and gently they will do their best.

The tallest flowers sway in the breeze
Scattering pollen that makes us sneeze,
Pansies with faces that seem to please
New hawthorn leaves, known as bread and cheese.

A snail - a slug - a little grey bug
A fly trapped in a web - gives a final tug,
A little frog sits under a stone
He doesn't mind if he sits alone.
In a pond nearby, his tadpoles have grown
You may hear him croak, but you won't hear him moan.
So, don't be bored my little one
With so much to see, it's so much fun
A new tale to tell when each day is done
Let Britain in the 3rd millennium
Bring days like these to everyone.

Margaret Suffolk

THE MILLENNIUM

The millennium came, the millennium
went without a hitch, or so we think,
There were all different tales of what could
go wrong; a shortage of water, a nuclear bomb.
The whole world awaited the stroke of
midnight, at all different times of our day
and night.
The world celebrated, the skies were aglow
all faces were shining with joy and much hope.
Our hopes for the future are so plain
to see, to make peace and goodwill a reality.
For each person in the World, this
millennium is our last.
For everyone of us who celebrated; it is now
our past.
Now we must look forward to a brand
new century,
A world so full of peace and love, how
wonderful it would be.

Dianne Pike

2030

Genetic disorders have now been irradicated
How?
By cloning perfect humans
DNA perfect that is.
We now have chromosome Z
This is neither male nor female.
Sex has been banned due to genetic disorders occurring
But let's face it we're better off without it.

Without sex;
No more paedophiles, no more rapists,
No government sleaze,
No gays, no prostitutes, no lesbians
No male, no female.
Future babies are clones with X or Y replaced by Z
Therefore not male or female
Non-sexual.
Mankind will be equal.

Babies are grown in womb *like* sacs of flesh
With perfect placenta and blood supply,
This eliminates the passing of blood disease,
Such as aids, hepatitis, haemophilia,
And of course future adults will have no wombs.
We look towards a perfect future of equality,
No more abortions, no more sexual crime,
No more pregnancies or labour to fund.
No more broken marriages, no more marriage.
We are all single people bringing up perfect children.
In a hundred years time people won't know what male and female are.

C D Tubbs

BALDHEADED INTO YK3

Two thousand years gone and into millennium three
Man's greatest achievements chronicled for all to see.

But if in perspective, man's discoveries are viewed all round
One perceives a cure for his baldness has never yet been found

Countless patent remedies have been applied to his pate -
Yielding hardly a whisker to show to his mate.

Treacles and juices from every type of loam
Have been rubbed, massaged, injected and planted on
His venerable dome - to no effect!

Bald and shining, reflective as a lamp
A tonsorial wilderness has made its stamp.

Outrageous displays of wiggery revealed to the world as fake
When the wearer faces moderate winds
Or takes a swim in the lake . . .

It surely never needs Sexton Blake to detect
The baldness of this rake.

Isolated transplants fail to project him baldly winning
When it's obvious to any onlookers that his locks are
                              depleted and thinning.

So heed you well this millennium plea.
Please find a cure for baldness by the end of YK3!

Roger N Colling

WAITING FOR THE GHOST OF SUNRISE 2999 CE

Midsummer Eve and they come they gather horde on horde
round plas-stone circle New Stonehenge
has filled space was Trafalgar Square
needed since outland too wild to go in
or safe bits not let without that pass
only billions can buy to pass Privsec Guard

will howlcrysqawkbaamoocawcacklebarkmiaow
these genemix people will lash tails shake
manes flap wings all up at fullbright moon
where promise is to them their queen looks
down and cares who went to be safe up there
gone with the colony of Best of Brits

pushed out when the floods came in for good
over fen and lowland coast hamlet town and
malaria came and such warmtime things and
new lands up there seemed better place and
no one can tell ignoring domes bigger n
better by far than crumbledown millennium one

megatentacle-cum-mammoth-bred superhuman
Prime Monster rules new marsh-and-sea realm
from up there in Tranquillitas Mare that
New London isn't just as good as old only
smaller and up there by law all stay full
human no more admixing off other species

DNA allowed not even for gifts of beauty
redoubled extra breasts or tails to lure
fur to caress or wonders of low-grav
flight wing-gift none of that not like
is for these left-homes here who howl up
up between the stones 'Oh mighty monarch, *care for us!*'

Steve Sneyd

2000 Years

Fireworks flare
Rockets zoom
2000 sparks light up the gloom
Faces turn upwards towards the sky
2000 years has just passed by

An angel on a journey smiles
A message I bring in form of a child
Do not forget what millennium means
A birthday of a supreme being

They spend millions on a useless Dome
When we have people in need of a home
Did they not think of the need of others
After all they are our brothers

The next thousand years
Will see an end to all our fears
With automation everywhere
And robots seeing to all our cares

Perhaps machines will get it right
Where men have failed
They just might
Stop the wars and grant us peace
The message that the angel brought
I could be wrong, it's just a thought.

Marion Joyce

NORMAL LIFE '99

Waking up, December the thirtieth,
With two days to go in this second millennium,
And then in with the third, and on,
And on. Hung-over from last night,
When I sat with my brothers,
Drinking. Now my mouth is dry
As a desert bone from a past civilisation,
And I get up and go to the bathroom
For a drink. As my body awakens,
I piece together the acts of the fore-night,
When we sat like the Vikings
A thousand years ago,
Drinking. Death-bounded,
With all that that brings, we escaped
From the worries and toils
That every Adam-man will carry
On his shoulders through time.
After a bowl of 'All-Wheat', my stomach
Content again, I go out to work,
To drive my heavy plough through the rain,
To ply my anvil of necessity
In order to carry on through the seasons,
And on. And tomorrow
We will celebrate the 'New Year's Eve'
As if it were some joyous prelude
To a new age. But the plough and anvil
Will not rust through under-use,
As we will drive and ply through time.

Rhys Thomas

DEATH IN THE FINAL CITY

Silver spires, solid concrete
Bright lights dark where subways meet
Processed air, no roads to cross
Identity cards, numbers embossed
One steel corridor encloses mankind
To train the thoughts, to close the mind
Perfect harmony, no jobs, no goals
The following of pre-ordained roles.
The city harsh and unforgiving
Where thousands earn their daily living
Blackened buildings, tortured spires
No one knows, no desires
One voice alone to my mind
A dweller follows close behind
Paranoia, persecution
All support my one illusion.
Death in the final city
Images bright and appealing
Designed to sell, not to tell
The harshness of reality
The mind spirals mental circles
Breakdown circuits once repairable
Incomplete, unnecessary, but desirable
A lasting death, the final parable.

M Stone

LET IT GO

In this persistent distress
what else but dissent
when limbs fly
babies cry
mothers die?

What land is this
which needs bloodied soil
to pave its toil
and build kingdoms of its dead?

Love chose the nourished soul
thus let it go

Have we forgotten
a mother's love would not consent
would not accept
the king's offer to recompense
with half her child's flesh?*

There is no compensation
for life wrenched.
No promised dream's revelation
in the hopeful eyes of infants
drenched red.
No Rightful Kingdom soars
from the cinders of the dead.

* Kings 3: Solomon's Judgement

Elizabeth E. Picard

The Washing Machine

The mangle won't work said my mum to my dad,
I can't do the washing, no clean clothes to be had.
My dad said I'll fix it with some grease and some oil,
So he set about taking the mangle to toil.
There were cog wheels here, and cog wheels there,
Dad didn't see me throw one in the air.
My dad got himself in a mess and a tangle,
Because he couldn't fix that dratted mangle.
So there hangs the story of mum's new machine.
The washing all done and spotlessly clean.

J Stuart

MILLENNIUM SATURDAY

In the year of your Lords, this first millennium
day. I have watched your last pass with much
distaste and fear.

Your past, your future so many times does it recur,
yet unheard, unlearnt, never undone

The last millennium, so bloody and brutal.
So full of hate and avarice. You rape your
mother with ever-increasing haste, you despoil
her love but still you spill her life bloody.
You reap the harvest of her bosom, but yet
lay waste her womb.

In this year of millennium began, will your
harvest of blood be less and of the land, will
it know less despoiling by human hand.
By act of war, of the human cost will your
Cenotaph's grow more and before you journey
this millennium new, think twice did the good
done out way the bad, of millennium past.

A S C Smart

As I Look Back

I look back across the years dear Lord,
there, so often I can see.
When I was a child so lonely,
so full of misery.
It was then I found you Lord,
You listened to my tale of wow.
It was you who helped me,
showed me which way to go.
You gave me imagination,
so that I could be.
Anywhere or anything I wanted,
as long as you were there with me.
And as the years went flying by
at unrelenting speed,
I left my childhood dreams behind,
but Lord I still had a need.
I needed you so much to share
my hopes and all my joys.
To thank you for my blessings,
when I had my little boys.
Then I lost you along the way,
I had no time for prayer.
Soon tragedy and pain so bad,
I cried, and you were there.
My Lord, my rock, my comfort
along this stony road.
How could I do without you
who bares my heavy load.

Irene Keeling

Nostradamus Said (?)

I, back in 1984
Was hoping for a Third World War.
In '99 the world should end
(This waiting drives me round the bend!)

Catastrophes don't come on time,
Like buses running three in line;
I sit and twiddle both my thumbs,
But Armageddon never comes!

Anthony Manville

MILLENNIUM

One last embrace;
The hand of history holds fast
Upon a fading century,
Reluctant to release a friend,
An ally. Side by side they journeyed
Through man's inventory;

Ever watchful,
Yet never to approve or disapprove,
Never to intrude,
An opinion never ventured, never sought,
Of man benign -
Whose wisdom bought a life,
Or warring man -
Whose arrogance defiled one.

Soon space will separate them,
For clocks pierce time with steady, even beats,
Shrill, staccato,
Relentless, unstoppable,
Towards the next millennium,
When old and new combine,

Converge, in one smooth dovetail of time;
One century, fastened safely to another,
With no seam the eye can see;
Where new hopes hold old fears at bay.

Man's legacy, written on a century -
Gold dust, or rust?
Both may blow as one,
When powdered by the savage wind of time!

Elaine Johns

The Breaking Day

There is a moment when the way ahead
Looks inviting, as though blue skies
Might always be filled with sunshine instead
Of the promise of rain or storm-surprise.
Maybe it's when the year begins
Or when hope wins
The battle to guide your heart.

There are also moments when what's gone before
Seems more than nostalgic. The past
Has its own magic and its colours gleam more
It seems that when it was new and looked to be made to last.
Maybe it's when the year ends
Or when memory lends
Enchantment to deceive your heart.

To look backward shows the way
To look forward in hope to the breaking day.

S V Batten

MY THOUGHTS FOR THE MILLENNIUM

What does the future hold in store?
Gloom and doom! And much, much more!
Will we be happy? Will we be sad?
Will events happen to make us glad?

Will inventions be made more marvellous still
Than ever we've seen or can imagine?
Will the thoughts of man transcend to Heaven?
Will we give to others, as we've been given?

Will we kill and steal and fight?
Or will we care, share and do right?
Will we learn to love our fellow men
Will peace ever prevail in the world again?

I know what I would like to see
A world of peace and harmony
With no more worry and no more care
A world whose bounty all men will share.

As I sit awhile and ponder
It is then I begin to wonder
If any of these will ever come
They are just some of my thoughts for
Millennium!

Mary Hellard Eastwood

What Does It Mean For You?

A new millennium, Y2K,
Another event, another day,
Great big world, starting again,
Sorting it out, ending the pain,
Making it new, getting it right,
But what does it mean for you?

There've been
Earthquakes and famines, plagues and rats,
Training of dogs, taming of cats,
Floods and volcanoes, no distinction,
Birds and insects achieving extinction,
Rainforest growing, rainforest going,
But what does it mean for you?

There've been
New popes and bishops, religious disasters,
Leaders and tyrants, vicars and pastors,
Empires born, countries wiped out,
A ride on the national roundabout,
Lands rearranged, identities changed,
But what does it mean for you?

Attempts to reduce the racial tension,
Demos' and dying, too much to mention,
Political parties, some still afloat,
Welfare and pensions, and women can vote!
Fashion and diets, reform and riots,
But what does it mean for you?

Health and humanity, people live longer,
Building and breaking, technology stronger,
Knowledge and learning, people earn more,
High unemployment, people are poor,
People run better, escaping disaster,
Sport is exploding, people fight faster,
Sex and drugs and Rock 'n Roll,
But what does it mean for you?

Timothy Paton

MY HOPES FOR THE NEW MILLENNIUM

Peace in the Third World
Money for them too
All these politicians
Working for me and you.

Stop all this fighting
It really is cruel
They'll end up like Oliver
Eating lumpy gruel.

The Amazon rainforest
Is being cut down
But do we really need
Another industrial town.

Cars cause pollution
They make you feel ill
So if you just keep on walking
We'll keep the environment still.

All of these things
And lots more too
The happiness of the whole world
Depends on me and you.

Kirsty Sellar (15)

HOPE
(Honour - Others - Pleasant - Existence)

To awake and find it's Jan the first,
Mouth like the desert, head waiting to burst,
Feeling sorry, bedraggled and glum,
Then you remember *Millennium's come.*
Run to the bathroom, scrub off the fur, run out and bellow
Happy New Year.
Forget resolutions, be human again, jump in a mudbath, or sing
In the rain. Laugh till you're helpless or even in pain.
Spare a few seconds, say *How doo-you-doo.*
Whilst rushing at top speed to arrive at the loo!
Sitting so tranquil, a smile on your chops,
Don't be afraid of those almighty plops.
Your innards are working, expelling the gas,
It's probably normal - a blast from the past.
But the turn of the fingers on old London's Big Ben
At the countdown we waited to all start again.
With joy in our hearts, and glass in the hand,
Off went the fireworks so high up above,
Parting the clouds, on a journey of love.
Whilst here on the ground, we stared in amazement,
The planning and sharing, fulfilment, the awe
We *all* have that chance to try even more.
So reach for the future, the *millennium's landed*
And so my friends move forwards,
Don't let yourselves get stranded.
Like an island surrounded by water for miles,
Reach for your dreams and hurdle those styles.
Believe in yourself and show us those smiles,
Just part the lips as you part the waves,
And I'm sure - sure you'll meet such better days.
Goodbye for now and good luck to you all,
Oh! And remember to *always walk tall.*

J Daintree

MILLENNIUM

Ring out the bells for this the third millennium.
Raise high your brimming glasses of champagne.
Greet one another with joyous affection,
Link arms and sing *For Auld Lang Syne* again.

What will the future bring
When all the revelry is through?
Will there be lasting peace on earth
And joy and love and brotherhood?

Will everyone forget their quarrelling
Their jealousy and greed and spite?
Will nations stop fighting one another
And live in harmony and joy and light?

And here in Britain will we see
The forest glades grow tall again
And foxgloves, rose and primrose grow
In every leafy country lane?

Or will the countryside be raped,
Car parks, towns, factories grow and grow
Until the fox, badger, mouse and vole
Become endangered species, having nowhere else to go?

Will otters live in rivers clean?
Will there be hedges where the bees
And butterflies can stay and feed?
Will birds still nest in leafy trees?

Will we have any choice at all,
And will the bickering cease?
Surely the whole world must unite
And this millennium bring peace.

Ann Linney

A Vision Of The Future

Long live our country
And the vision we have for thee
Of the onward march of history
As we build a new society
With human values, where each is free
To be who they want to be.

In the quest for reality
We must be superstition free
There is no God and we have no soul, you see
They're an idealist fallacy
A reflection of our conscious fears from history
Where justice and truth are fettered by gold and brutality
As greed is hailed as ideology
And ignorance and bourgeois notions masquerade as philosophy.

With a pride in who we be
We salute those in history
Who struggled for equality
Not for you and not for me
That can never be
But to save the world and humanity
From the tyranny of wage slavery.

J Paton

Looking Forward

We're looking toward the future
to the new millennium
with excitement and trepidation
in awe of what is to come

Shall we save our planet for
future generations to enjoy
or will our new technology
be used to destroy?

We must think very carefully
about the years ahead,
to learn to live unselfishly
for when all is done and said,
our actions now will mean so much
throughout the future years
for we need to bring peace and happiness
not pain suffering and tears

Jenny Brownjohn

ARROWS

And will our feet in future time
Walk upon England's mountains green?
And will the butterfly and bee
In hedge and meadow still be seen?
And will the woodlands in the spring
Be carpeted in bluebell blue?
And will the skylark sing?

I will not cease from mental fight
Nor shall my pen sleep in my hand,
'Till we have saved our trees from blight
And firmly stand.

Freda Hendry

GREAT BRITISH OAK

Great British Oak, stand tall in the forest of humanity.
Each sunrise of the new millennium sends rays of hope
                                          and possibilities.
Harsh forces of world conflict shake your branches, causing leaves
                                          to fall,
But the light of each new dawn finds you standing fresh and strong.

Great British Oak, be proud of what you are.
Your old gnarled branches give form and structure from the past,
Young stems and fresh new buds offer promise of life to come,
That which is neither supports the whole and ensures continuity.

Great British Oak, you must be nurtured.
Care must be taken to nourish you, great giant, feed the roots well.
Investment and encouragement for progress are essential,
Beware of the many parasites waiting to strip away your very heart.

Great British Oak, there is always a future.
Should lightning forces knock you to the ground
Dormant acorns lie ready to spring into life.
Your form will be admired for centuries to come.

Great British Oak, do not compete with nature.
There may be bleak long winters to come, times may be hard.
As you cast your coat of gold to the wind,
Know that spring will soon lift your spirit and renew your soul.

Great British Oak, no other can compare.
Steeped in history, with great opportunity to come.
Always be powerful, stand firm and proud.
The future is good in this new millennium.

Angeline Laidler

Y2K

Am I in an alien country,
Foreign language everywhere?
They're not speaking Esperanto
Or a dialect that is rare.

They are talking log on, dot com.,
What the hell does all that mean?
Web sites, internets and surfing,
Maybe I am in a dream.

Now my grandson's speaking to me,
Where's his e-mail, where's his mouse?
Get some cheese and ask the Postman,
He's just hurried past the house.

Find my daughter in the kitchen,
Weighing kilos to make bread,
Adds a litre to the mixture,
Await the outcome with some dread.

TV's blaring, no one's watching,
G.M. Farming's caused a rage.
Man has cloned a sheep called Dolly,
B.S.E. has made front page.

Change the channel. It's a Clinic.
Transplant organs from a pig.
Choice of implants or a facelift,
Tummy tucks, perhaps a wig.

Can I cope with all these changes?
Do I want to? I'm not sure.
Give me peace and understanding,
After all I'm ninety four!

Sheila Colling

Millennium

A bright shining diamond that graced ancient skies
Giving light to the birth of a very special child
Whose life was to follow a true path that defies
The old ways and those who were against peace beguiled

The world then was not willing and able to believe
That there was one good and kind soul that could be
With an honest intention and pledge not to deceive
And then only after a cruel death would they then see

That this world could be such a good and peaceful place
Where one man is able to survive along with all other man
In a state of companionship and tranquil calm ways
And try to continue the great journey that he began

And as time has now passed two thousand years
There have been those of wicked and evil intent
Who have tragically spilled so many innocent tears
As against his good work their defiance was spent

L J Edwards

HIGH STREET 2100

Thermalizers on boys - we're going to the urban gigastore
Oh get real dad, go on-line there're bargains there galore
Electric mail and surfing won't find what I must buy
I need to see, I need to smell, I am a touchy feely guy

So we arrive in our helipod to a concrete Cathedral on top of a hill
Where robotic assistants spill out their spiel
Dad can we have two mill for the Orgasmatron.
No! You're not old enough.
Get down to the clone zone Hitler's strutting his stuff

Couldn't find what I came for, let's get ourselves home
And let's stop for a litre in that new Alchodrome,
Dad we're both starving those organic burgers smell nice
You'll have Mcmodified nuggets there at least half the price

Paul Edwards

THE CHILDREN DID PLAY - 1930'S

Back in the days when we were young
Not much money but we still had fun
The games we played kept us fit
No time then to brood and sit
Beneath the skies of blue or grey
The children did play

The fun cost very little at all
With lots of pleasure from a bat and ball
A top and whip, a length of rope
And imagination to give us scope
We used it well in every way
That's how the children did play

But mams and dads, God rest their souls
Had no hope then to reach their goals
Men longed to work, if only they could
Women stretched pennies for rent and food
Yet through the hardships of each day
They were pleased the children did play

Sadly it took a war to erase
The age of depression and poverty days
And what a price the world would pay
With millions of lives along the way
Yet spirits prevailed, come what may
And through it the children did play

Now the new millennium is here
We pray for a future that's bright and clear
Answers to problems hopefully found
For the year 2000 many dreams abound
It's time for the world to find a way
So that all the children can play

Gloria Aldred Knighting

WE WHO DREAM

we who dream
draw straight
lines
on white paper
in the daytime

at night
we send
squiggles
over rainbows

to and fro

and smile
to each other
in the dark

Sandy Lunoe

SUBMISSIONS INVITED
SOMETHING FOR EVERYONE

POETRY NOW 2000 - Any subject, any style, any time.

WOMENSWORDS 2000 - Strictly women, have your say the female way!

STRONGWORDS 2000 - Warning! Age restriction, must be between 16-24, opinionated and have strong views. (Not for the faint-hearted)

All poems no longer than 30 lines.
Always welcome! No fee!
Cash Prizes to be won!

Mark your envelope (eg *Poetry Now*) *2000*
Send to:
Forward Press Ltd
Remus House, Coltsfoot Drive,
Woodston,
Peterborough, PE2 9JX

**OVER £10,000 POETRY PRIZES
TO BE WON!**

Judging will take place in October 2000

Dead Edward

Stephen Moore

Hodder Children's Books

a division of Hodder Headline Limited

CORNWALL COUNTY LIBRARY	
JF	05-Mar-02
£4.99	PETERS

Copyright © 2001 Stephen Moore

First published in Great Britain in 2001
by Hodder Children's Books
as part of Hodder Silver Series

The right of Stephen Moore to be identified as the Author
of this Work has been asserted by him in accordance with the
Copyright, Designs and Patents Act 1988.

10 9 8 7 6 5 4 3 2 1

All rights reserved. No part of this publication may be
reproduced, stored in a retrieval system, or transmitted,
in any form or by any means without the prior written
permission of the publisher, nor be otherwise circulated
in any form of binding or cover other than that in which
it is published and without a similar condition being
imposed on the subsequent purchaser.

All characters in this publication are fictitious and any resemblance
to real persons, living or dead, is purely coincidental.

A Catalogue record for this book is available
from the British Library

ISBN 0 340 74396 4

Typeset by Avon Dataset Ltd, Bidford-on-Avon, Warks

Printed and bound in Great Britain by
The Guernsey Press Co. Ltd, Channel Isles

Hodder Children's Books
A Division of Hodder Headline Limited
338 Euston Road
London NW1 3BH

Contents

PART ONE: EDWARD ON THE INSIDE

1	Things That Go Bump in the Night	3
2	Light in the Darkness	8
3	Sticky-tacky Puddles	16
4	The Trouble with Eternity	27
5	Mr Tuddle	35
6	The House of the Humble Dead	39
7	Dinner with the Pattinsons	49
8	Home Truths	54
9	Haunts and Haunting	59
10	Tap, Tap, Tap	64

PART TWO: EDWARD ON THE OUTSIDE

11	The Silence of a Memory	73
12	The Ghost Town	82
13	The Hawker	91
14	A Matter of Possession	99

PART THREE: EDWARD ON THE OTHER SIDE

15	Dispossession	109
16	Awkward Questions	116
17	Fireworks	119
18	Lies	127
19	Out on the Streets with Mildred	132
20	The Stuff of Life	138
21	Second Thoughts	144
22	A Moment Too Late	147

Postmortem   153

Part One
EDWARD ON THE INSIDE

ONE

Things That Go Bump in the Night

My name is Edward. Edward Gwyn Williams. I'm a school boy. I'm fourteen years old, near enough. Let me tell you something—

I will *always* be a school boy.

I will *always* be fourteen years old.

I AM DEAD.

Edward Gwyn Williams is dead.

Yes. As surely as flesh rots and dry old bones are dry old bones, I am stone dead. A ghost, a phantom, a spirit. You can call me what you like, but call me dead.

Now, that's not said to worry you, and it's not said to scare you stiff – though perhaps it might – it's only said to let you know the facts of it. Yes, the facts.

You see, I've got a story to tell you. My story. Not the story of my life. Heavens, no! But the story of my death. And, more importantly, the story of what became of me *afterwards*.

First though, a word of warning. Take heed.

Dying is easy. Dying is all *too* easy. *Anybody* can do it, and undoubtedly will. It's only a matter of time, a question of when and where and how. So mind you don't go looking for death, life's too short for that, too precious. Believe you me. I know.

That said . . .

How did I come to be dead?

How did Edward Gwyn Williams die?

I was at home. I tripped down the staircase on my way to the toilet. Don't laugh at me. It's not meant to be funny.

The month was October – late October. It was the middle of a freezing cold night. I remember, there was rain. There was rain banging as hard as ice cubes against my bedroom window. Out in the back garden, a howling wind was kicking up a fuss among the plastic dustbins. Turning them over, stealing their lids, tumbling them noisily down the garden path. (That's probably what woke me up in the first place.)

I suppose I should have clicked on a light as I jumped out of bed, but I'd come instantly awake and was instantly bursting with it. You'll know that feeling? I was desperate for the toilet, and was already halfway across the landing before I realised it was pitch dark.

Too late.

It was there I fell over Guy Fawkes. You know? The Guy Fawkes I'd been making for Bonfire Night out of my dad's old jacket and my mum's old tights stuffed full of newspapers. I'd left him sitting on the landing windowsill for safe keeping.

He must have fallen off, because he wasn't on the windowsill now. He was lying in the middle of the landing floor, hidden in the dark, perfectly positioned to trip me up and throw me head first down the stairs.

I fell in slow motion. Or at least, it felt like slow motion. Over and over I tumbled, falling forever in the darkness. And as I fell Guy Fawkes fell with me. His cloth arms wrapped tightly about my legs.

Then— Thump! (That must have been me hitting the bannister or the stairs.)

Thump! Bump! Snap! Crack!

Sounds too close to the noise of breaking bones to be anything else.

There was no pain with it though. Odd that. There was never any pain. None that I can remember, that is.

And as I fell in the darkness my mind's eye began to play silly tricks on me, showing me flashes of things I could not possibly be seeing for real.

Flash!—

There was our house. Our big, ugly old monster of a house. Number thirteen, City Road. Perched on top of the hill. Above the town. The thing was, I was on the outside now. On the outside of the house looking down on it, as if I was floating about in the night sky. I could see its blackened chimney pots and its roof tops glistening wet, though I couldn't feel the rain.

Flash!—

Floating higher still. Far, far below me I could see a curling river set deep in its valley, and splashed with electric light reflected off the street signs of the town. Further away, was a darker dry valley where a motorway ran off into the countryside.

Flash!—

Close to the house again. Only I was looking in through an upstairs window. I could see the outlines of familiar bedroom furniture. Against a wall I could make out an ancient iron radiator (it was banging and rattling, making a terrible fuss).

Flash!—

Now a different scene. I could see Glynis Chapman – not my girlfriend – just a lass from up our street. She was standing in her garden next to her back door, and suddenly bathed in brilliant sunshine.

Then – *Flash!*—

Something real again. All too real. A sudden stillness in the dark. I'd stopped falling. I was lying upside down at the bottom of the staircase. I could hear the rain beating against the hall window. I could smell the stale dusty smell of the hall carpet.

Then, from somewhere in the darkness, I heard a voice. An anxious, a naked, squealing voice. It was calling out to me.

'Edward? Our Edward, is that you?' It could have been my mum, but my mum in tears. Or else it was my sister, Aggie?

'What's happened? What's going on? Where are y—'

The voice stopped in mid-sentence. It did not fade away

or echo into silence. It simply stopped, and I never heard it again. Not ever.

In that same moment *everything* stopped.

And *nothingness* became everything...

TWO

Light in the Darkness

Do you know what? When you're dead you know you're dead. Don't ask me how you know, you just do. It's the same as when you're alive – you know you're alive. Nobody has to tell you about it. So, there was no doubt. I knew I had died. The trouble is, when you're very first dead, you simply don't believe it. Or rather . . . Rather, you don't *want* to believe it.

I mean, who in their right mind would want to end their life where I'd just ended mine? My life had hardly begun. I had ambitions. I had plans. I had a future. And I had a great long list (incomplete!) of *Things I Really Must Get Around To Doing Very Soon.*

1. I hadn't finished my maths homework.
2. I hadn't flown in an aeroplane.
3. I hadn't watched *half* the videos I'd recorded off the telly.
4. I hadn't even been drunk (not what you could call *properly* drunk).

5. And as for girlfriends! Well, I hadn't . . . You know, I just hadn't.
6. Do I need to go on . . . ?

And fair enough, my list might read like nothing very spectacular to you, but try looking at it again from my point of view. I'm fourteen years old and my list of *Things I Really Must Get Around To Doing Very Soon*, had suddenly and irreversibly turned into my list of *Things I Won't Ever Be Doing!*

How long the *nothingness* went on for I couldn't say. When I came to myself it was completely dark, though some sense told me I was still lying at the bottom of the staircase at home. Number thirteen, City Road. I remembered the fall. The terrible fall . . . Had it been bad enough to kill me? I mean, if it had killed me, where was my poor broken body? Where were my family? Why weren't my mum and my dad weeping and wailing? Why wasn't my sister, Aggie sobbing her heart out? And where were the angels? Where was the bright light, and all that other magic stuff, to show me the way up to Heaven?

Let me tell you, there was none of it. Only the dark. The never-ending, the unchanging dark. No shadows. No form. Not even the dim light of the street lamps seeping in through the hall window to bring relief.

And in that dark there was a silence. An utter, a complete silence. No wind blew. No rain pelted the windows. I couldn't hear the sound of my own breath!

Breath?

'Hu— Hu— Hu—' I tried it. I wasn't breathing.

I wasn't breathing. I wasn't hurting. I couldn't see. I didn't even want to go to the toilet!

I tried breathing again.

'Hu— Hu— Hu—'

I thought really hard about breathing until, to my relief, I felt my chest rising, lifting and falling as it filled up with air. Or so I thought.

I relaxed a little. That was a mistake. As soon as I stopped concentrating my breathing simply stopped too. And I couldn't get it going again.

As I lay there, alone in the dark, I tried to make sense of it all, when there wasn't any sense. (Well, not if I wasn't ready to believe the simple truth ... that I was dead!) I began making up excuses. The whole thing was obviously a horrible nightmare. That's all. Either that, or maybe, just maybe, I really had fallen head first down the stairs and was at that very moment lying in a hospital bed in the deepest of comas.

I tried pinching myself awake. I dug my nails in hard, enough to bruise my skin black and blue, the way the rude lads at school pinch the bums of the girls in the dinner queue to make them squeal, but nothing happened. I wasn't even certain I felt it!

To be honest with you, I was beginning to get scared. I stood up. I wobbled uneasily to my feet. I tried to take a step in the dark. That was another serious mistake. It was my body that was the problem. You see, there was no proper physical sense of weight or movement to it. And I was definitely feeling less than solid. A whole lot less than solid!

I panicked. I stretched out what I hoped were fingers, searching the darkness for anything that might be familiar, only to draw them back again. *What if I really was dead?* (I was still arguing the point.) What if I'd become some kind of ghost? Surely, my fingers would simply pass right through anything I tried to touch? Wasn't that how it worked?

I had to prove it to myself. One way or the other. I struck out hard, repeatedly slapped at the darkness with the flat of my hand, until I knew I'd hit something. A wall? To my relief the wall stayed solid and firm under my hand.

After that I took things a lot more carefully. I walked my fingers slowly across the wall. I touched what felt like a picture frame under my fingers. I found a wall lamp with a shade over an electric light bulb, and a switch. I tried the switch. The lamp didn't work.

'I wish you were a real light.' It was only a thought, spoken on the inside of my head. Not words, out loud. But something very odd happened. Out of the darkness a light flickered. It flashed momentarily, burned feebly, withered and died.

Astonished, I repeated my thoughts. I kept them on the inside of my head. 'I wish, I wish you were a real light . . .' Again a flicker of pale light broke the darkness. It was as if my thoughts were something real, that could be carried through the darkness to light the lamp. This time, as the light withered, it did not die. Not quite. I began to realise, the more I concentrated, the harder I tried, the better the light glowed. The more fiercely it burned.

There's something you need to know about that light. I understand it now, though of course I didn't then. It wasn't the light of the wall lamp shining. There wasn't a light bulb flickering in the dark. In fact light is probably the wrong word for it altogether. You see, when you're dead there is no light. Not what you or I would call real light. There is no sun. There is no moon. There are no candles to burn down. There is no electricity to power a sixty watt bulb. No. There is only weird-light. Spectral-light. The light that belongs to the dead. The light that belongs to the things of the dead.

The wall lamp was showing itself to me because I wanted to see it there. And the more I wanted to see – the more I tried desperately to see – the more I began to see.

Gradually the spectral-light spread out along the wall. It moved across the passageway in one direction and crept up the staircase in another. Soon I could make out the hall window and the long mirror that hung on the wall close by, even see as far as the front door.

What was being revealed to me there would have taken my breath away, if I'd had the breath to take away.

Was this really number thirteen, City Road? Was it?

I recognised Guy Fawkes. He was lying in a crumpled heap on the hall floor, exactly where he had fallen. His arms – the arms of my dad's old jacket – were caught underneath him, and his stuffed-tights head was thrown back. I could see the silly toothy grin I'd drawn on his face with a fat felt-tip pen. He looked just the way he was supposed to look, if strangely colourless . . .

(That was something else I had to get used to. Death has no colour – just as it has no light – or at least, little enough colour to speak of. Only the black of darkness. Only the drab grey tones of spectral-light, sometimes tinged with a morbid luminous blue-green, giving shape and form to the objects it clings to.)

In life, the carpet Guy Fawkes was lying on was a plain and simple purple, almost brand new. Now it too had lost its colour and was an endless, toneless grey. Worse still, as the carpet began to climb the stairs it also lost its newness, lost its plainness, and became instead, a worn out old rag covered in a swirl of ugly-looking drab grey flowers.

It made no sense. But then, what did?

Half way up the staircase the wooden bannister simply stopped being made of wood and turned into black wrought iron. Two steps higher and the stairs themselves split in two. One set kept going the way they had always gone and managed to reach the top, but the other took a sharp turn to the right and buried themselves in the solid wall.

And if the front door was still reassuringly, recognisably mine, I could not say the same about the other closed doors I could see. The dining-room door had obviously been badly scorched by fire; its paint was blistered and peeling. While the living-room door had an old-fashioned, round brass handle that hung down sadly from its spindle, as if it might not be attached to the knob on the far side.

But forget the doors. There's more nonsense upon nonsense. Take a look along the hallway behind me. The kitchen, and the whole back end of the house had vanished behind a monstrous slab of bare stone wall that grew up through the floor and disappeared into the ceiling. That stone wall might well have belonged on the side of a church or a castle maybe, but it did not belong there.

And where there was not something unusual to see, there was nothing to see. And I do mean, there was *nothing to see*.

There were wide gaps in the walls and in the floor and in the ceiling with *nothing* between them. Not an empty nothing full of holes; a solid nothing, a smooth, an impenetrable nothing, that could be touched, that could be felt, but never passed through. (Believe me, I tried.)

Confused, I turned to the hall window. I peered out through the glass, searching the darkness there for something I might recognise, something I could more easily understand than all this.

There was only more nothing. Endless nothing. And whether it was solid and touchable or just an ordinary dark empty space I couldn't tell.

I stayed at the window. Kept on staring and staring, and hoping . . . and hoping. And in the end I did see something out there, at least I think I did. Something vague, something distant. Was there spectral-light, breaking into the darkness outside? Maybe.

Though I'll tell you what there wasn't. There wasn't a single reflection, or a shadow. There wasn't a moon, or a star-flecked night sky. There wasn't a wind or rain or rumbling storm clouds. In fact, there was no weather at all.

Then it struck me . . . I had seen the last of weather.

There was going to be no more weather for Edward Gwyn Williams.

THREE

Sticky-tacky Puddles

I turned away from the hall window and found myself looking instead, into the hall mirror. I don't think I had purposefully avoided the mirror – or maybe I had? Anyway, there I was looking back at myself. Dead Edward. Sort of grey, tinged with morbid blue. Sort of vague and shimmery. Only the ghost of an image. Of course, it would be the ghost of an image, wouldn't it? I didn't know whether to laugh or to cry. (I didn't even know if I *could* laugh or cry.)

I turned away from the mirror. Only to turn back again. Dead Edward.

I was still wearing the clothes I'd gone to bed in . . . the clothes I had died in. I always slept in a scruffy T-shirt. That night I'd chosen the one I'd made in my art lesson at school, for the 'Fighting For a Fairer World' project. On the front I had drawn a globe – the world – and encircling it, I had printed my slogan: *I don't want it all, but a little bit would be nice.* (I'd made that up myself.) Below the T-shirt I could see a pair of yesterday's underpants. Below them were two skinny legs complete with school socks, and – on my feet – my sister's fluffy slippers. I'd forgotten all about our Aggie's fluffy slippers. I'd borrowed them ages ago – without asking of course. (Well, you don't do you?) I couldn't find mine, and well . . . I *had* meant to give her them back. I only wanted them for the middle of the night. Nobody else was ever going to know about them. Were they?

I'll tell you, if I wasn't already dead I'd have been dying of embarrassment! Whatever else was wrong with being a Dead Edward – and there was plenty – this was definitely no way to dress for all eternity.

Fortunately, I didn't have long to worry about it, because just about then, something even more extraordinary happened.

At the very ends of my fingers and in the gaps between my toes an odd, sticky liquid was beginning to gather. It formed into droplets. And before I knew it, there was a puddle beneath my feet, around my sister's fluffy slippers. It was a pale, a glowing, a sticky-tacky puddle; and the same funny-peculiar grey colour as my reflection in the hall mirror.

Instinctively, I tried to lift my feet out of it, but the puddle only stretched and pulled and came with me, like liquid chewing gum.

I took a giant step along the hall, as if I could walk my way out of it. The puddle only followed after me. I put my foot on the bottom rung of the staircase and began to climb. The puddle climbed too. What was worse, the sticky-tacky puddle was slowly growing. It was spreading out all around me.

I put my feet together and leapt down from the stairs. I jumped as far as I could possibly go, this time convinced I had left the puddle behind me. Though the moment my feet touched the floor, there it was, gathering around them again. And the puddle was growing more quickly now.

I could not think why it was happening. I did not know what it was. I watched as the puddle began to seep into the hall carpet. I watched as it formed into tiny streams that ran underneath the skirting boards and spilled into the gaps between the floorboards.

Not surprisingly, it was quite some time before I became aware of the cat . . .

I don't know where the cat came from. There didn't seem to be anywhere it could have come from. At home we didn't own a cat. But there it was, all the same, crouched with its back to the dining-room door.

It was a small, a scrawny-looking creature. A common moggie. And although it was wearing a kind of handmade leather collar it had more the look of a wild animal, than a pet.

The cat began to lap enthusiastically at *my* sticky-tacky puddle.

I watched it for a while, unsure of what else to do.

Shouldn't I have been annoyed, or shocked? In a way, I felt rather pleased. Glad of the company. Well, it hadn't exactly been much fun up to now – being dead on my own.

Then the thought struck me, and like a thunderbolt – Of course! If I was a ghost, then surely the scrawny cat was a ghost too!

I took a closer look. Just like me the ghost cat wasn't quite solid enough to be anything else, especially about its legs and along the length of its tail. And it had the same ghostly-grey colour tinged with blue-green.

'Here, puss-puss-puss,' I gave a gentle, encouraging hiss (hoping I still had a voice to hiss with).

The cat ignored my call.

Somebody else didn't!

'Oh, Mildred! What do you think you're doing? You cruel thing! You know that's not fair!'

The voice was loud and it was angry, and it was coming from up above me. Had the angels come to collect me after all?

I looked up. Stared.

Standing on the landing at the very top of the staircase was a girl. She was smaller than me, and at a guess, could have been no more than ten or eleven years old.

She was no angel. But she was nobody I knew either. This just had to be another ghost.

I couldn't stop staring. The girl was wearing a full length dress buttoned to the neck, and a bib and apron like an old-fashioned servant, or a Victorian chambermaid. Only her hair looked wrong. It was long and wiry, and it was sticking up on end (which made me wonder if she had died in the middle of combing it). In her arms she was cradling a wooden toy, and – as I was beginning to understand – like me, she wasn't *quite* solid.

That didn't stop her from thumping her feet noisily as she came down the stairs.

'And why are you letting her do it, you stupid boy?'

I didn't answer. Only continued to stare. I hadn't a clue what she was yelling about.

'Go *away* Mildred. Shoo! Shoo!' The girl skirted past me and, careful not to stand in the sticky-tacky puddle, aimed her foot at the crouching cat's backside.

'Miaow!' Mildred did not wait for contact. The cat hurled herself up the stairs, only stopping at the top to hiss and spit her annoyance at us. Then she turned away, scooted out of sight, and I forgot about her.

With Mildred gone, the small girl turned her full attention to me. She looked me up and down in a very curious way, scowled and then – of all things – she gave a reluctant curtsy.

'How do you do,' she said, politely. (Though in a tone of voice that didn't quite match.) 'My name is Beatrice. Beatrice Tanner (1901). And I hope you don't mind, but I've been watching.'

'Beatrice? 1901? Watching?' Actually, I did mind. But she wasn't making a lot of sense to me, so I let it pass.

'Yes. My haunt's just at the top of the stairs – along the landing. So it's not like I was being a nosey. I only came out when I saw you were in trouble.'

'Your haunt? Trouble?' She still wasn't making a lot of sense.

'Yes, well. I'm surprised you've managed to last as long as you have. There are as many new 'uns as don't, you know.'

'What? Sorry?'

'Ghosts,' she said, as if that explained it. 'Ghosts.' She waggled a finger at me. 'Just take a look at yourself. You're leaking. You're leaking everywhere!'

'Leaking?'

Beatrice raised an eyebrow at me. 'And will you please stop gawping at me like a goldfish, repeating every last thing I say. It's not polite. You're beginning to sound like an echo!'

'Ech— Oh, I'm sorry, but, but— Hang on! What am *I* saying sorry for?' I'd suddenly remembered – I might be a ghost, but I was standing in front of a strange girl dressed in only a T-shirt, a pair of worn nylon underpants, and with our Aggie's fluffy slippers on my feet! '*You're* the one who's come thumping down *my* stairs, bursting into *my* house uninvited.'

'*Your* house?' Beatrice raised her other eyebrow at me. It was quite some look. Like a sneer but with nails in it. And I had to admit – what with the stairs splitting into two and disappearing into the wall, the peculiar looking doors and the stone wall sitting in the middle of the hall – she did have a point.

'Look,' I said, 'I'm having a crisis here. I'm in a state of shock. It might have escaped your notice but I've only just died. Just this very moment fallen down the stairs and killed myself. This is not one of your run of-the-mill bad days. This is as bad as they come! And I'm in no mood for a lecture from someone who looks like my great grandmother's baby sister.'

I thought I'd put her well in her place. Beatrice only looked at me, blinked slowly once, and then pointed at the floor.

'If we don't do something about *that*, and quickly, there'll be an awful lot more to worry about than dying . . .'

The sticky-tacky puddle around my feet was turning into a lake.

'I was just going to ask you about that,' I said, trying to sound as if I wasn't really bothered about it one way or the other. 'What . . . What exactly is it, then?'

Beatrice closed her eyes and winced, hugging her wooden toy tightly to herself. She looked as if she was getting ready to explode. I'll swear, her wiry hair suddenly stood upright, and something – something that looked very much like an outbreak of nits – began to hop and leap about.

'Oh, you would think *someone* would tell them the rules, *before* they got here!'

I don't think she was talking to me.

Beatrice opened her eyes and pointed at the wall. 'You had better take a proper look at yourself in the mirror.'

'I've already done that,' I said, offhand. But she spoke in such an abrupt, bossy way, I found myself doing it anyway.

'Oh— !' It was like looking at a shadow. It was like looking at the ghost of a shadow. Or should I say, the shadow of a ghost? I was still all there, as it were – there was nothing missing. But I'd become so terribly transparent, I reminded myself of a dirty glass milk bottle.

I looked into the mirror. I looked at Beatrice. I looked

back into the mirror. I looked at the puddle on the floor. 'Beatrice—? What's happening to me?'

'Please— Just do exactly as I tell you. We've got to stop your leak, or else— Or else—'

'Or else?' I looked straight at her, but she avoided my eyes. There was something she desperately wanted to tell me, only she didn't know how.

'Listen. To be a ghost you have to ... you have to concentrate on being a ghost. You have to think about it really, really hard. And if you don't ... If you don't, you— you—' She stopped there and looked anxiously down at the puddle around my feet. So I finished her words for her.

'You leak? You leak out all over the hall carpet?'

'Fwut!' she said, with a wave of her arms that needed no explanation. 'Fwut!'

The little bit of me that was still me began to feel very unusual. Not ill, worse than ill.

'How do I stop it, Beatrice?'

'Like I said. You must think. Concentrate on *being*. You're dead now. Dead! A ghost doesn't have a real, live body. But you *can* keep your ghostly, spirit body – if you try hard enough.'

'So you mean this sticky-tacky liquid stuff is part of ... ME?'

'Yes. It's the very *essence* of your being.'

'My what?'

'Your *Essence of Being!* It's what ghosts are made of, silly.

And you can't afford to lose any! You're already beginning to fade! Understand?'

'Oh—'

'Ghosts aren't flesh and blood. They don't have arms, they don't have legs to stand on. You haven't got ears or eyes or a nose or a mouth or . . . or *anything*. Not really. So, you have to . . . Well, you have to *think* them into shape – and you can't do that without Essence of Being!' She was sounding more and more urgent. She dropped her wooden toy on the floor and clasped her arms tightly about herself. 'And when you've got your shape, you must hold your spirit body firmly together with your thoughts. You must never forget who you were in life— Who you are! Remember the way you looked. Remember what it was like to move about, to touch, to feel, to *be* . . .'

I didn't think I could possibly remember so many things at once. But I wasn't in any position to argue. I closed my eyes and tried to concentrate. Then I remembered what she'd just said – that in all probability I didn't have any eyes, and that only confused me some more.

'Stop frowning, and think positively,' said Beatrice. 'Think about who you are. And how it felt, being you. Quickly, before your Essence leaks away altogether!'

I was still frowning. What she was asking wasn't easy. Learning to think yourself together, when you've always had a perfectly good body to do the job for you, isn't.

'And your name. What's your name, boy?' she demanded. 'Tell me your name!'

'Er . . . it's Edward.'

'Then you must say it. Say it out loud. And believe in it!'

'Edward,' I repeated, but it came out rather too feebly. I had *meant* to shout, only my voice seemed to be draining away along with the rest of me.

'Try again!' said Beatrice.

'Edward. I am Edward.'

'Oh, you'll have to do a lot better than that!'

With my eyes tight shut, I tried to gather my thoughts together, and to think even harder. I thought about my arms stretching out into the air. I thought about my head thrown back towards the sky and my lungs so full of wind they were near to bursting. Until at last—

'I AM EDWARD GWYN WILLIAMS!' I roared. I was yelling at the very top of my voice.

For some moments nothing seemed to happen. Until I felt the slightest of trickling sensations in my ghostly toes and legs. The faintest of tingling glows at the ends of my ghostly fingers.

I yelled again. 'I AM EDWARD GWYN WILLIAMS (2000)!'

There came the strangest of sensations – a rumbling, a gulping, a gurgling rush. I felt as if I was being engulfed by a warm ocean wave – only it was filling me up on the *inside*.

'Yes. Yes! It's worked!' Beatrice cried excitedly, clapping her hands together with delight. 'Look Edward. Look!'

Cautiously, I opened my eyes. The sticky-tacky puddle around my feet had gone.

I studied my hands. I held them up to my face. They were solid. They were real. So were my legs! So was my body! So was . . . everything! (Well, they were all as near solid and as near real as a ghost was ever going to get.)

I gave Beatrice a hug then. I couldn't stop myself.

Afterwards, there was a sort of embarrassed silence that neither of us knew how to fill. I didn't know what to say. I wasn't used to eleven-year-old girls. Least of all, ones who've been dead for nigh on a hundred years.

Beatrice was standing with her head on one side. She had picked up her wooden toy and was quietly nursing it. She had stopped being Bossy Boots and become just a little girl again.

'Is that . . . *thing* a doll?' I asked. It wasn't what I wanted to ask. There was a whole pile of unanswered questions stuffing up my head. But well, I couldn't think.

Beatrice shook her head. 'No, silly. It's a tiger.'

'Oh,' I said. It didn't look much like a tiger (maybe a cat at a pinch!). It had a few hand-painted stripes on it. But it was little more than a roughly cut block of wood with rag and peg legs.

'By the way . . . Thanks, Beatrice. You know . . . Thanks for saving my life and that.'

She didn't look up, but I'd give you a hundred pounds to a penny she smiled.

'I didn't save your life, Edward. You're not alive.'

'All right, then. Thanks for saving my death . . .'

FOUR

The Trouble with Eternity

How can I put this tactfully? I can't.

So . . .

When you're alive, it's safe to assume that one day you will simply stop being alive. Do you get my meaning? You live – you die. It's inevitable. The same for everyone; if a rather sad fact of life that's best not dwelt upon. But I never thought, not once in all my born days, that I would be facing the same anxiety about being dead. I assumed that dead was dead and that was that. And once you were safely dead you stayed that way. There was no if or but or maybe about it.

Well, how wrong can you be? Here I was, with the breath hardly out of my body and a mere novice of a ghost, and I was already struggling to keep myself that way. Look at the facts. They're grim reading:

A) I was – most definitely – dead.
B) Death – it appears – does *not* last for ever.

Just as Beatrice said. A ghost that can't think, that can't

hold its spirit body together with its thoughts, simply leaks out all over the hall carpet. Their Essence of Being drains away to nothing. They go off fwut! Put it how you like, but it brings us to the inevitable, and unavoidable conclusion, that:

C) Eternity is not . . . Well, is *not* eternal.

Can you believe it? I don't think even I fully understood the implications of it just then. I hadn't quite grasped what it might mean for me, or for any other ghost come to that. (Or maybe, I didn't really want to understand?) Anyway, if you're looking for a problem to solve you're hardly going to find a bigger one! And so it was.

After Beatrice saved my death, she left me on my own again. Not maliciously. There's just something in the nature of house ghosts. They don't like to be away from the safety and comfort of their own haunts for longer than is strictly necessary. They don't like the unknown. They don't like change. It kind of scares them. And to Beatrice *I* was the unknown, *I* was change.

Without a word, she started up the stairs and, not knowing any better, I started up after her, only to have her turn back and stop me half way.

'No, silly!' She tut-tutted. 'You must wait here, Edward. The bottom of the stairs is your haunt.'

'Is it?'

'Yes, of course. That's where you died! And I'm only

going for a . . . for a *rest*.' There was an almost whimsical look about her as she spoke, and I could tell by the way she said *rest*, that it wasn't the word she was looking for.

'But, Beatrice—'

'I'll come back again. I promise . . . And next time I'll fetch Mr Tuddle with me.'

'What?' The mention of another name came as quite a shock. I'd had just about enough of puzzles. 'Beatrice, who's Mr Tuddle?'

'Oh, Mr Tuddle's a Professor. At least we all call him Professor. He knows just about *everything* about *everything*. This house. This world. Ghosts and all that. He likes to think he's in charge too, but he's not really. He's just been around a lot longer than anyone else.'

'Anyone else?' I couldn't believe what I was hearing. 'You mean he's another ghost? And there are *more* ghosts in the house?'

Beatrice only laughed. 'Well of course, Edward. You didn't think we were the only ones ever to have died here, did you?'

'Well, no I suppose not, but—' It wasn't a very comfortable thing to think about.

'Listen, I won't be away for long—'

'But—'

There was no point in me arguing. At that she was gone, climbing up the stairs, disappearing along the landing.

I did as I was told. I climbed back down to the bottom of the staircase and waited there for her.

Waited . . .

★ ★ ★

Time . . . Now, there's a funny thing. Or maybe it's not such a funny thing when your time has run out? You see, I was about to make yet another peculiar discovery . . .

When you're dead there is *no time!* (You know, of the tick tock, tick tock, variety.) That makes it extremely difficult for a ghost to know how long *anything* actually takes. Do you understand? Without time, how do you tell how long it is between one thing happening and the next thing happening?

For example, Beatrice told me she wouldn't be away for long. But exactly how long did I have to wait for her at the bottom of the stairs?

I don't know! That's the truth.

Was it a few seconds, or minutes? Hours, or days?

Did time pass slowly or quickly? If there was no time, did time pass at all? When I think about it, however long it was it never really *felt* as if time was passing. All I can say for certain is that there *was* a gap between Beatrice going away and her coming back again.

How can I be so sure?

Something happened. Something horrible.

After a while (and please *do* notice how good I'm getting at being totally noncommittal about periods of time). *After a while*, of just generally hanging around at the bottom of the stairs, I noticed the tiniest of sticky-tacky puddles gathering around my feet. So, with nothing else to do, I decided I'd better put in some practice at holding my spirit body together with my thoughts. I started with the basics. I repeated my *I am Edward* routine just as I'd done with Beatrice. And once I was convinced that I could, as it were, think-myself-together without having to worry about small, embarrassing leaks, I began to experiment. I tried doing two things at once.

Like, thinking-myself-together and walking up and down the hallway. Like, thinking-myself-together and taking off my sister's fluffy slippers, putting them on again. Like, thinking-myself-together while thinking about something entirely different at the same time. That was hardest to do of all. (You should try it, you'll soon see what I mean.) It's like being stuck in the middle of two separate conversations – both of them going on inside your head.

I did manage to do it in the end, though not without a struggle. And if now, it all comes to me like second nature, it certainly didn't then. What I got wrong, what I got seriously wrong, was the subject I chose to think about . . .

My family. My living family. You know . . . *Before*.

That was my mistake.

My mum and my dad, and our Aggie. Though admittedly, it was mostly our Aggie. She's a couple of years older than me, and not bad as far as sisters go. Aggie's her nickname. It's Maggie for real. When I was a baby I could never quite get my tongue around the 'M' so it always came out as Aggie. The name just stuck. (It's funny the things you do remember.) The trouble began when I tried to think of her in any more detail than that. I couldn't. I just couldn't. There was a sort of fuggy mist getting in the way inside my head. I couldn't make out the details of her face (I couldn't make out *any* of my family's faces.) Inside my head I spoke to her, and I'm sure she spoke back, but I couldn't hear her voice, not clearly. The harder I tried the more difficult it became. The mist inside my head turned into a swirling fog. It blotted out everything, carrying them all further and further away from me. I tried to follow after them. I wanted to follow. I wanted to go with them. Only now, I was lost in the fog too, and I knew that wherever they were I could not possibly reach them.

And the feelings ... The dreadful wash of feelings. Sorrow. Fear. Despair. But do you know which was the worst? It was homesickness. Yes, homesickness. So deep. So terrifying. I'd never, never ever felt anything like that before.

Did I cry out loud? Or was it just inside my head? I don't know.

I suddenly realised, I was no longer alone at the bottom of the stairs.

I'd been surrounded ... by ghosts. There was a small crowd. A mass of faces. Five or six or seven. And they were concerned, worried-looking, grey faces, but with a kind of warmth, a glow about them that was not matched by their sad expressions. Among them, voices were anxiously murmuring.

'Well I never did, Mother. What do we have here, then?'
'A new 'un, do you think?'

'Aye, Father. Aye. And not long over, I shouldn't doubt.'

'He was making such an awful noise!'

'The poor soul.'

'You know how it is, lass. It's always the innocents who are the first to suffer.'

'Aye, aye—'

As the voices chuntered on, heads nodded or shook in solemn agreement. Then they seemed to sense that I knew they were there, and the faces drew back.

Surprisingly, they moved as a crowd. Not one at a time. Not even one after the other. But together. And all together they moved back towards the dining-room door – the door that was burnt with the blistered paint. Only now it was standing open.

Their movement let me get a better look at them. And I realised, they weren't so much a crowd as, well . . . They reminded me of an old-fashioned black and white family photograph. There was a mother and a father, and there were children. And they were all dressed up like a posh Sunday, with jackets and ties and summer dresses. Polished shoes, stiff hair-dos and leather handbags.

I wanted to say something, so I said, 'Hello.'

There was a slight gasp and together the family looked guiltily towards the staircase, as if they were making certain no one else was listening.

'Hello, lad,' whispered the father. He leaned towards me. (And as he did, his whole family leaned with him.) 'Pattinson's the name. Pattinson (1953) . . . We just thought we'd better pop our heads round the door. Thought you might be in a spot of bother, like?' He paused, briefly. 'But it's the er . . . the Professor, see. He don't like us talking to the new 'uns. Not first, anyhow. Not without him having made the proper introductions. It's on account of . . . Well, he likes to think . . .' He stopped there. All the faces were looking at each other. Was it a smile or a grimace? I couldn't tell.

'He likes to think he's in charge?' I offered, finishing his sentence for him.

'Aye. Aye, summat like that, lad. And you know, we don't like to upset the old fella, not at his time of death. So, if there's nothing amiss, we'll say no more about it, eh? That's for the best. Say no more about it.' All the heads nodded together in agreement.

I was curious, I wanted to know more. I needed to know more. But the next moment there was another slight, collective gasp and then a sort of rumbling swishing noise, like the gentle swell of a wave or the whisper of a breeze through a bank of grass. Then as one the family of ghosts glided in through the open dining-room doorway, quickly pulling the door closed behind them.

Something on the stairs had startled them.

FIVE

Mr Tuddle

Standing at the top of the stairs was Beatrice. She wasn't alone. Next to her stood a crooked old man. Or rather, the ghost of a crooked old man. Beatrice grinned down at me and waved, (and I'm sure, pretended she hadn't just seen the dining-room door close). It was the old ghost who spoke first, and he spoke as if he already knew me.

'Edward? Is that Edward?'

I knew instantly I was going to like him.

He began making his way down the stairs. He walked sideways, labouring over every step, taking each of them deliberately and carefully, one at a time. Too carefully almost, the way that some very old people do – like they're made of fragile bone china and might tip over and break themselves. (It puzzled me. *Can* a ghost fall and hurt himself?) Beatrice followed quietly after him.

'Edward Gwyn Williams?' As he spoke his presence seemed to fill up the house, at odds with the frailty of his form. The spectral-light began to glow more intensely; the vague, darkest corners of the house seemed less vague, less dark.

'Yes,' I answered him. 'I am Edward.'

The old ghost began to chuckle. 'Splendid. Splendid. You are Edward Gwyn Williams (2000) and I . . . I, young sir, am Cornelious Tuddle (1856). Who is most pleased – nay, sir – who is most delighted to make of your acquaintance.' He had a voice that, for some reason, reminded me of school. School and dusty old books in Year Six English lessons.

When, at last, he reached the foot of the stairs he took my hand in both of his and shook it. His touch was so slight it felt like a kissing breeze. (I decided, maybe a ghost can be *too* perfect. I mean, just look at how well Mr Tuddle had remembered himself from his final moments of life. His aged body, his crooked stoop, right down to the very last fragile detail.)

'Aren't you the er . . . the Professor?' I said, not knowing what I should say. I tried to give Beatrice a quizzical, in-need-of-help look, but she wouldn't look back at me.

'Professor, young sir? Professor?' I thought he looked seriously worried for a moment, almost annoyed, but then he seemed to change his mind and was chuckling again. 'Ah – now isn't that a splendid title – Professor! But alas, it is not an appendage to which I can make any but a false claim. A title which is – shall we say – one of our young Beatrice's common amusements.' He turned and gave her a narrow look I could not quite read.

It was only now, close up – through the warm glow of his

spectral-light – that I took particular notice of his strange clothes. Most spectacular was the tall top hat he was carrying under one arm. His jacket was as long as an overcoat, with a collar that stood up at the front and tails that hung down at the back. His trousers seemed too tight and too short for his bandy legs, and showed his knee-length stockings underneath. None of his clothes looked new. To be honest, none of them looked as if they had ever been new.

'Edward Gwyn Williams,' Mr Tuddle repeated to himself, as if he was clarifying the facts. (And I nodded, but I don't think I needed to.) 'Now then, young sir, let me see— You are, perhaps, still feeling a little on the – shall we say – the shocked side? Nay! Bemused? Nay! Perplexed?'

'Well I—'

'Indeed. Indeed. Of course you are. Newly arrived! Newly arrived – it is only to be expected.' He began to pace very, very slowly up and down the hallway, always stopping and turning, just before his nose bumped into the great stone wall. 'Though we must not worry ourselves unduly, eh? We'll soon have you sorted out. Filled in. Brought up to the mark! The very epitome of a *house ghost*, eh, Beatrice?' Again, he gave Beatrice a look I could not quite read.

Mr Tuddle continued vaguely, 'The question is . . . The question is . . .' He hesitated, and stood perfectly still with one, paper-thin finger raised towards me.

'The question is?'

'Where?'

'Pardon?'

'Where, young sir. Yes yes. One might suppose that the beginning would be the very place? Or perhaps that should be the end?' He grinned through a mouth full of broken teeth. 'There will be, questions to answer? And – I have no doubt – answers to question?'

I nodded enthusiastically, replied too quickly, 'I do have *some* questions. There's all that messy, leaky-puddle business. And the strange dark nothingness outside the hall window. And well, I still don't understand what's happened to my house?'

From the vacant look on his face, I wasn't certain Mr Tuddle was listening, until he threw my last words back at me. '*My* house? *My* house?' It might have been an accusation.

He began pacing up and down again, though more quickly now. He was forgetting his own frailty. 'But such an inquiring mind. Indeed. Such an inquiring mind.' He tapped his chin with his finger, and then opened his arms and with a swish of his top hat made a huge sweeping gesture. 'Come. Come young sir, follow after me. Let me show you *our* house. This house of the humble dead. And all will be revealed. Eh, Beatrice? All will surely be revealed.'

What else could I do? I followed after him.

SIX

The House of the Humble Dead

Mr Tuddle – with Beatrice always at his side – led me slowly and methodically all through the house of the humble dead. I tried to believe all the things he told me were true, that all the things he showed me were real, but it wasn't easy. And I'm not at all certain that he began with the bedrooms, or that he ended where we'd first met at the bottom of the stairs, but that's how I remember it now.

The upstairs of the house was much the same as the downstairs of the house. Namely – except for my small corner at the bottom of the stairs, where Guy Fawkes was sitting propped up against the wall, next to the front door – I didn't recognise any of it. None of it seemed to belong to my house. Number thirteen, City Road. The house I'd once lived in. There were long passages with twists and turns in them that did not belong. There were walls with far too many doors in them. There were walls with no doors in them, where there should have been doors. And here and there, where there should at least have been walls, there were only smooth black areas of solid, impenetrable nothingness.

'Notice the exquisite period details, young sir,' said Mr Tuddle, sounding rather like a tour guide. He ran his fingers down the wall at the exact point at which an oil painting of a ship under full sail, had been cut neatly in half. It ended suddenly, and turned miraculously into a photograph of a very stiff looking King George VI. 'See how beautifully, how effortlessly each manifestation blends into the next. That sir, is craftsmanship of the highest order. Nay, of a by-gone era—'

'Manifestation?' I interrupted. I had to know what he meant by it.

Mr Tuddle, cut off in full stride, looked mournfully at Beatrice.

'Edward doesn't fully understand,' she said.

'Ah, quite. Quite!' He turned to me. 'Young sir. You are at least aware – as it were – of your, your . . .' He drew a vague circle in the air with his finger as if it would help him find the word he was looking for.

'Condition?' suggested Beatrice.

'Indeed. Your condition— ?'

I nodded. And as I did, Mr Tuddle nodded with me, though he was looking inquisitively at Beatrice.

'Edward knows he's dead,' she said.

'He knows he's dead. Quite . . .' Mr Tuddle stood quietly for a moment, collecting his thoughts. Then he was striding purposefully up and down the landing with one finger held aloft.

'Manifestation, young sir, manifestation is soon explained. Let me see ... When any living creature dies, be they a man of learning (er ... like myself) or a mere humble maid-servant (like our young Beatrice here), they each bring to this world of spirit any part of their immediate physical surroundings which still bear those final traces of their life. Those close personal items which hold the very essence of those last few precious moments.'

He spun about on the spot and with a flourish pushed open the nearest door. 'For example! I, young sir, I died here, in this very room.'

Behind the door it wasn't a bedroom, it was an office. And it was far too long and far too wide an office to truly belong behind the wall where it now stood. The walls and ceiling were panelled oak. In one corner there was a rather creepy display of stuffed animals – a grinning fox and a prancing rabbit that both looked the worse for wear. There were endless bookshelves crammed full of books. And in the middle of the floor there was a huge wooden desk strewn with papers. There was a carriage clock and an inkwell, and ink pens made out of feathers.

Mr Tuddle wasn't finished there. He beckoned me to follow him to the far end of the landing, where a small wooden stool stood in a corner on its own, lost in the shadows. 'On the other hand – alas – young Beatrice here, has only her corner, her three-legged stool and her toys.' At which point Beatrice gave a rather forced, self-conscious curtsy and held out her wood and rag tiger as if it was an exhibit.

Luckily, I was beginning to understand what this all meant, which was just as well because both Mr Tuddle and Beatrice were looking at me in a very expectant manner.

'And I died when I fell down the stairs. So I have my front hall, my T-shirt and underpants, a pair of my sister's fluffy slippers and Guy Fawkes.'

'Quite! Quite! I think he's got it. Eh, Beatrice?'

Beatrice nodded enthusiastically.

'And it all appears just as it was at the *very* moment each of us died? Like a snap-shot? A stolen moment in time?'

More enthusiastic nodding.

'And *that's* why the house is such a jumbled up, higgledy-piggledy mis-match of everything?'

'Nail on the head, young fellow-me-lad! Nail on the head!' At that, Mr Tuddle took Beatrice by the hand and led her a jig along the landing. You couldn't have helped but laugh.

That house tour was the strangest mix of wondrous joys and poignant sadness. Mr Tuddle led us past a long line of closed doors. He stopped at each one in turn, taking hold of the handle and pulling on it. They were all locked. When he next spoke it was in a hushed whisper.

'There are ghosts among us, young sir, who – shall we say – prefer the pleasure of their own company.'

'He means they don't ever come out!' interrupted Beatrice.

'Eh?'

'Quite! Quite! Solitude and loneliness is their lot. They are such heady idealists.'

'Such ridiculous barmpots, you mean,' said Beatrice.

Other doors stood purposefully ajar, and the rooms behind them were very much occupied.

In one bedroom there was a middle-aged man wearing a pair of striped pyjamas together with – of all things – an old tin army helmet. He was sitting up in bed quietly playing a game of solitaire which was balanced on his knee. The room was dark and austere. There were thick black curtains at the window and one small bedside table lamp which was giving off only the tiniest of spectral-glows.

'This is Mr Andrews (1940),' said Mr Tuddle, shaking his head. 'He is a sad, sad victim of war.'

'Oh!' I said.

'No he isn't,' said Beatrice. 'He's a grumpy old moaner, who never gets out of his bed. And he didn't die in the Blitz or anything. It was a heart attack.' She didn't bother to whisper, but Mr Andrews wasn't taking any notice of us anyway.

In the bathroom there was a young woman who couldn't have been much older than my sister, and appeared to be crying into a mirror. She was wearing white plastic knee-length boots and a very short dress that was printed with a swirly, black and white pattern (that hurt your eyes if you stared at it for too long).

'This is our Charlotte (1967),' said Mr Tuddle.

'Hello, Professor. Hello, Beatrice,' said Charlotte, in a slow, tired, squeaky sort of voice, and without taking her watery eyes off the mirror. She didn't move until Mr Tuddle introduced me, and even then she only turned her head and added, 'Hello, Edward.'

She was heavily tear-stained and her make-up had run, leaving thick black lines of smudgy eye shadow all over her face. Charlotte had obviously died looking that way, and as no one else seemed to think it was the least bit unusual I didn't say anything. At least not until we were walking away. Then I asked, 'Why is Charlotte crying?'

'Oh, Charlotte is *always* crying,' said Beatrice, unsympathetically. 'She's very good at crying for a ghost.'

'Indeed, indeed,' agreed Mr Tuddle. 'In life, Charlotte was a . . . was a . . . How can I put it?'

'Was a very emotional young woman,' said Beatrice.

'Ah yes. Quite so. Quite so. A very emotional young woman.'

'And how exactly did she come to die in a bathroom?' I asked.

Mr Tuddle began to cough theatrically. 'Died of a broken heart.'

'She's a suicide,' muttered Beatrice, hurriedly. 'Her fiancé ran away to Blackpool with her best friend and never came back. But it's not something she likes us to talk about . . .'

'Oh—'

In another room there were two small children, little more than toddlers, happily playing on the floor with their toys. Behind them, was a woman dressed in a posh, floor-length evening gown – she was standing near the window reading a letter. In one corner sat a whimpering dog and in another what looked like a very fat rat. The odd thing was, none of these ghosts was paying the slightest bit of attention to the others.

I couldn't help but be curious, and I must have been looking puzzled because Mr Tuddle began shaking his head at me, as if he understood my bewilderment. 'Alas. Poor nameless lost souls . . .'

'Sorry?'

'Oh, this lot are worse than Mr Andrews,' said Beatrice. They looked it. 'And it's not so much that they're nameless, it's more that we can't *ever* get a word out of them. You see, they don't believe they're here. We can't get them to understand that they're dead.'

After the lost souls, I was pleased to get back down the stairs.

The great stone wall that had sprung up in place of the kitchen turned out to be something of a mystery, because it didn't seem to belong to anyone.

'Ah, now this is a most interesting manifestation,' said Mr Tuddle. 'A most interesting manifestation! Note how beautifully, how precisely each of its stones has been cut almost to a regular square. And though I have seen neither hide nor hair of any ghost to prove my theories, I have little doubt young sir, indeed I am certain – this wall is Roman, and of some great antiquity.' He puffed out his chest, wanted me to be impressed.

In a way I was, only there was something slightly puzzling about his explanation. 'Yes, but surely . . . if this wall's a ghostly manifestation then it *must* have a ghost of its own?'

Mr Tuddle seemed to visibly deflate. He looked sharply at Beatrice.

'Edward, it doesn't work like that,' she said.

'Doesn't it?'

'No. A manifestation needs a ghost to bring it into our world, but once it's here, well, it's here to stay.'

'You mean,' I hesitated. 'Even if its ghost goes off fwut?'

'Yes.'

'Wow.'

The front room was even less promising than the Roman wall. I tried turning the brass handle on its door and it came off in my hand. 'Um . . . It won't open?'

'Quite. Quite—' said Mr Tuddle, moving straight on to the dining-room door.

I looked quizzically at Beatrice.

'*Of course* it won't open, Edward,' she said. 'There's *nothing* behind it.'

'Right!' I said. I think I was finally getting the hang of things.

'Now come on, let's go and meet the Pattinsons, I just know you'll like the Pattinsons.' (Beatrice gave me a wink). 'They haunt the dining-room.'

Mr Tuddle tapped politely on the dinning-room door. It was answered immediately, as if the knock had been long expected, and a whole host of voices chorused together,

'Come in.' For no reason that I could think of, I found myself smiling.

The door swung open and there were the Pattinsons standing together in a line, exactly as I had last seen them. Only now there was a peculiar, vacant expression on their faces. I soon realised why. They were trying to pretend they had never seen me before. (Though there were knowing sneaky nods in my direction.) Mr Tuddle was beaming with delight.

'Now young sir, let me introduce you to the Pattinsons, the Pattinsons (1953)!'

Mr Pattinson leaned towards me (his whole family leant with him) he took hold of my hand and, giving an exaggerated wink, shook it vigorously.

'Pleased to meet you, lad.'

'It's always nice to see a new face,' said Mrs Pattinson. 'And well – if our Beatrice hasn't come calling too. This your new young man, then? Your boyfriend is it? You were never a one for being backwards at coming forwards!'

'This is, Edward,' huffed Beatrice. 'Edward Gwyn Williams (2000). And he is *not* my boyfriend.'

There was a chorus of disbelieving laughter (it was then that I discovered ghosts can still blush).

The Pattinsons went on talking. Altogether, all at once, in their cheery sing-song way.

'And of course you'll *all* be staying for your dinner? In't that so, Mother?'

'We were just about to make a start, Father. So there's not

another word to be said on the matter.'

'Come on in. Sit yourselves down. Make yourselves at home.' We found ourselves being ushered quickly into the room.

'Eh, our Beatrice with a sweetheart. You'd best tell us all about it.'

'And give them a comfortable seat our Sydney. There'll be no standing on ceremonies in this house. What you see is what you get with the Pattinsons!'

It was.

SEVEN

Dinner with the Pattinsons

The dining-room was a large room. Even so, there was so much furniture crammed into it, I wondered how any one – even a family of ghosts – could find the space to move around. In the middle of the floor there was a large wooden table with nine chairs. It was set out for dinner, complete with food and drinks. Against one wall there was a saggy old sofa and against another two saggy old armchairs, all with worn leather covers and looking as if they'd been in just one too many fights with small boys. There was a bookcase, and a plain tiled fireplace with a gas fire apparently burning at full blast. In the bay window there stood an old-fashioned television set, with a flip up lid and a screen no bigger than a paperback novel. (It was rather like a blind man's dead eye, peering at us from the corner of the room.)

Then there were the Pattinsons themselves. I'd already met them once of course, but their appearance was no less remarkable the second time. Each of their faces had its own head, its own body, arms and legs, but there was something very different about the Pattinsons. Something was keeping them locked together, within the same spectral-light. They did not move about as six separate ghosts, but as one ghost. When Mr Pattinson walked over to the fireplace to fetch his pipe his family followed after him. When Mrs Pattinson led us to our seats at the dinner table, they all came too.

'A *Kindred Spirit*,' said Mr Tuddle, mysteriously, and he sounded most impressed. I wondered whether he should have spoken out so loudly, right there in front of them, but nobody seemed to be the least bit offended.

'And stop staring, Edward,' quipped Beatrice. 'It's rude.'

'Oh—'

'Now leave the lad be, Beatrice,' laughed Mr Pattinson. 'It's no secret. The Professor explained it to us, right enough. And a Kindred Spirit is what we are.'

He turned to me.

'That's to say, we all died together, lad. At the same moment like. It was a gas explosion. Way back in 1953. Just on dinner time and all, which was a stroke of good luck. And the family that dies together, haunts together, so to speak.'

'Aye, an' eats together too!' said Mrs Pattinson. 'So, stop your gabbing Father and let our guests eat up their dinner.'

'Oh, aye. Aye—'

At that the whole Pattinson family suddenly attacked the food on the table.

I picked up a knife and a fork, but I hesitated. 'Is it all right if I, if I eat it, Beatrice?'

'Oh, of course, silly. It's all part of their manifestation, in just the same way that Guy Fawkes is part of yours, and my tiger is part of mine.'

That meal looked as good as Christmas. There was a whole roast chicken with stuffing. There were roast potatoes and mashed potatoes. There were sprouts and carrots and parsnips, and home-made gravy. Although I have to admit, eating ghostly food isn't quite the same thing as eating food for real. It was all a kind of elaborate pretend. A sort of make believe. There were no enticing, mouthwatering smells, and I had to try and remember how everything tasted in real life to get the proper effect. (I ended up with more than one mouthful of mashed potato that felt like a wispy ball of cotton wool and tasted of dry dust.)

When the Pattinsons weren't eating, they were talking. And when they weren't eating or talking, they were laughing. You couldn't help but join in. It was a meal and a company I'm never likely to forget. Though what was stayed with me most clearly is the odd way the serving dishes instantly filled up again the moment we emptied them, the way the dirty dinner plates and the knives and the forks shone beautifully clean ready for the next meal, the moment we set them down.

'And don't you go filling yourselves up on too many Yorkshires,' said Mrs Pattinson. 'I've got a steaming bowl of home-made rice pudding for afters—'

'Aye, and it'll have a proper skin on it and all!' said Mr Pattinson, giving me a knowing nudge with his elbow.

'Home-made rice pudding?' Maybe being dead did have some compensations after all?

Unfortunately, I was counting my chickens before they were hatched. We never got the chance to try the rice pudding. Because it was then that it came, and without any warning.

Tap tap tap. Tap tap tap.

The knocking at the front door.

The change in that dining-room was instant. The laughter, the talking, the eating ceased. The meal was over. The room, the whole house, fell deathly still, deathly quiet. (The dead are particularly good at that kind of still, that kind of quiet.) If we had been breathing we would have stopped that too.

Tap tap tap. Tap tap tap.

There it was again.

I did not understand the reason for the sudden change in the house. I looked at Beatrice and Mr Tuddle in turn.

'Should I go and, and answer—'

The grave looks I got in return froze my words in my mouth before I could finish.

No ghost moved. Not for an age. Not until it was obvious the caller had given up and gone on their way.

Even then, no one would speak. I was quickly ushered out of the dining-room and the Pattinsons closed themselves in behind their door. Without a single word, Beatrice helped

Mr Tuddle climb back up the stairs to his office. They were both frantically keen to return to their own haunts, as if there was safety there.

But safety from what?

I was left all alone at the bottom of the stairs.

EIGHT

Home Truths

I could not settle to my haunt. Left to my own devices, I did not know what to do with myself. As far as I could see, ghosts don't really *do* very much. In fact, there doesn't seem to be anything very much they *can* do. Or, rather, there doesn't seem to be anything very much they *need* to do. So many of the things you take for granted when you're alive simply don't matter when you're dead.

The dead don't *need* to sleep. They don't *need* to eat, or drink, or breathe. Not being alive they don't *need* to go out to work to earn a living, and they don't *need* to stay at home to do the housework (because there isn't any). The dead don't *need* to use their eyes to see with, or their ears to hear with, or even their mouths to talk with. They may be what we're all used to – and most ghosts still prefer to do things the traditional *living* way, because it makes them feel better about themselves, somehow – but none of the things we do are strictly necessary.

Anyway, the gist of it is this: if you ever come across a

ghost of your own, you'll most likely find them just generally hanging about. Idly doing nothing in particular, vaguely *haunting* things. (And the only advantage to it, is that a ghost never *ever* gets bored with it. Getting bored, being something else that the dead don't *need* to do.)

I, on the other hand, still being something of a novice ghost, was having difficulties. Everything that had happened since the moment of my death kept coming back to me – going around and around and around inside my head.

There was my family. Our Aggie. Mum and Dad. Vague and more vague. And all but lost to me now. Lost, behind an ever darkening veil, in some secret, distant place I could no longer reach.

And there was this house. Number thirteen, City Road. What had it become, with its strange ghostly inhabitants? The house felt like ... Well, not like a home. No. It felt more like a cage than a sanctuary. Not a place of safety, but a prison! The world beyond that front door was not shut out. No. I – or rather we – we were all shut in.

If this really was all there was to eternity, then I was beginning to feel glad it wasn't about to last for ever.

I stared out through the hall window. Out into the darkness, out to where the nothingness was stained by the faintest glow of spectral-light.

I had to talk to Mr Tuddle again. I went up to his office uninvited, and I made Beatrice go with me, though I could tell she did not want to. I walked straight in.

Mr Tuddle was sitting at his desk, studying his papers. He

looked up. There was no surprise on his face. It was almost as if he had been expecting me.

'I want to know about the outside,' I said.

'Outside, young sir?'

'Yes. Outside of this house. *And* the callers at the door. I want you to explain them.'

Beatrice went and stood close to his desk. I was beginning to wonder whose side she was on.

'Edward, we don't go outside,' she said.

'Eh?'

'We're house ghosts.'

'What do you mean?'

'Oh, Edward! You're hardly cold in your grave and you already think you know it all!' Beatrice stamped her foot. 'We are house ghosts. *This* is our place. *This* is our haunt. Here we are safe. It's where we belong. And now it's where you belong, too.'

I couldn't believe what I was hearing. 'You mean to say, you don't ever go outside? Not ever? But there are lights, and, and—'

'Ah, the rashness of the newly deceased,' said Mr Tuddle. 'But you will begin to understand, given time. Given time—'

'Yes, well. That's something else I wanted to talk to you about—'

'And you wouldn't like it outside!' said Beatrice, deliberately putting herself between Mr Tuddle and myself. 'Listen to what the Professor's saying!'

'There are many ghosts abroad, young sir, some who – shall we say – it would be no privilege to meet.'

'There are ghosts who stalk the streets,' said Beatrice, theatrically, her eyes suddenly wide, 'in search of victims.'

'Indeed! Indeed there are!' Mr Tuddle forgot he was supposed to be a frail old ghost and jumped up out of his seat. 'Afrids we call them—'

'Afrids?'

'They are ghouls, malevolent spirits – and so sourly strong-willed.'

'Oh?'

'They prey upon the weak minded,' added Beatrice, trying to be helpful. 'The feeble of spirit.'

'Quite!' agreed Mr Tuddle. 'They prey upon any poor unfortunate soul less mindful than themselves. Believe me when I tell you, they are the devil's own kin! Scoundrels, hawkers, rogues all! They would barter for your very last breath if you had one! And what they did not care to barter for they would simply steal from you!'

'Oh yes? And what have I got to steal? I mean – just look at me!' There I was, standing in my underwear.

Mr Tuddle pushed his thumbs under the lapels of his jacket and puffed out his chest, as if he was addressing the entire house. 'What *has* he got to steal?'

'His very Essence,' said Beatrice in a very small voice. She turned to me. 'Essence of Being, Edward . . .'

I suddenly remembered Mildred, the ghost of the old cat licking at the sticky-tacky puddle around my feet. And I remembered the way Beatrice had come charging down the stairs to stop her. 'You mean they steal your, your . . .' I could hardly think it, never mind say it.

'Every last drop,' said Mr Tuddle. 'Until . . .'

'Fwut— !' said Beatrice.

(I was beginning to remember how to feel sick.)

Mr Tuddle started to pace gravely up and down behind his desk. 'Mark my words, young sir, and mark them well . . . We keep ourselves to ourselves in this house. Our windows are always locked tight shut, our doors are always firmly bolted. Alas, no world is a perfect world, not even this one. You would be wise to follow our example, it has served us well enough. And remember, *no* ghost may enter where they have not first been invited. An open door is as good as an invitation to an uninvited guest.'

At that, he sat down again, and began to shuffle through the papers on his desk. And that was an end of it. There was nothing more.

NINE

Haunts and Haunting

Beyond the hall window no rain ever fell, or dried up again.

Days never turned into nights. Nights never turned into days.

The sun never rose. The sun never set.

Seasons didn't come and seasons didn't go.

Nothing happened. *Nothing* changed. *Everything* stayed exactly the same.

Isn't there something to be said for a humdrum existence, where everything is ordered, ordinary and safe? That's how things are meant to be when you're an everyday house ghost.

You should be proud of me. I was finally getting used to being dead. And if I say so myself, I was even quite good at it. I could now sit quietly at my haunt for time without a measure (which of course it was) just endlessly doing nothing. And I was becoming ever more forgetful. Forgetful of my family. Forgetful of the living world on the other side. Forgetful too, of that other, odd business – with the caller at the front door. Whenever any of it tried to get inside my head I would let the woolly fog settle there instead – thick and impenetrable – until none of it seemed to be anything more than the vaguest of distant dreams.

Often, Beatrice would come and visit me at the bottom of the stairs, keeping me company – which, I have to admit, pleased me more each time. So much so, if she stayed away for too long I might find myself climbing the stairs to seek her out. It was rather like having a mixture of kid sister and friend, rolled up neatly into one. You know? We'd talk together, or just sit quietly, *haunting*.

What's haunting like? I'll tell you. In a way, it's quite nice really – once you get used to it. I suppose it must be similar to . . . fishing. In life I never did see the point in all that sitting around at the edge of a lake stuff. Spending hours and hours dipping sticks into pools of water, and not caring in the slightest whether you actually caught anything or not. But you know, I can see now that it must be a sort of peaceful, restful thing to do. It gives you the space to just *be*, to simply exist. Instead of having to be always rushing around *doing* things all the time – if you get my meaning. Anyway, haunting's the same sort of thing as that (though without the fish of course!).

Sometimes, when Beatrice and I were in a boisterous mood we'd invite ourselves for Sunday dinner with the Pattinsons. And if we were lucky, at the end, Mr Pattinson would let us choose a favourite book from their bookshelves and he would read it to us. (Yes! Every glorious last word!)

Other times, if we were feeling particularly brave

or mischievous, we would creep quietly along the upstairs landing and into the back bedroom, where we would secretly watch the crotchety Mr Andrews playing his game of solitaire. (Though along the way, we were always careful to avoid the row of locked doors and the open door with the poor lost souls behind it.)

Then there were our visits to Mr Tuddle's office. We'd usually find him sitting at his desk, with his head buried in his papers or scribbling furiously in his journals. We would always try and quiz him about what he was up to, though he would never give much away.

'What's the story today then, Professor?' I remember asking him once.

'Story, my boy? This is no story,' he began absent-mindedly and without lifting his eyes from his papers. 'I'm writing my new theory. I'm calling it *Possession* . . .'

'Possession?' asked Beatrice.

'Indeed. Indeed. That's an actual physical possession of an inanimate object by a ghost, to y—' He suddenly seemed to remember himself and stopped his explanation. Only to glance towards the corner of the room where he kept his stuffed fox and rabbit, and to add, mysteriously, 'There are some things, young sir, young miss, that are best left – shall we say – undisturbed?'

He carefully closed his latest journal before either of us could get a proper look. And well, if he wanted to keep his things private, let him. I was always more interested in the amazing carriage clock he kept on his desk. He'd explained that it was French, and something called a quarter repeater (I only knew it had the most beautiful chimes I've ever heard). Mr Tuddle liked his clock wound up regularly, so that he could pretend to be marking time for real. Though of course, he would often forget about it because time didn't really matter, and the clock would be left to run down. And when it was eventually wound up again its hands were allowed to carry on from the exact point at which they had left off!

However, I think if you were to ask me to chose my *most* favourite of times, they were the occasions when Beatrice managed to coax Charlotte away from her bathroom mirror. Charlotte had died aged seventeen, and that made her a real woman of the world in our eyes. She would dry her bleary tears, and begin telling us rude, grown-up jokes, or even ruder stories about the kinds of things she used to get up to with her fiancé. At which point Beatrice, being a bit of a Victorian prude, would put her hands up to her ears and pretend not to be listening. (Though of course she was really, because she didn't actually have to use her ears to listen.)

It was always during these conversations that the subject of life before death would come up.

'Don't *you* remember anything about your old life then, Beatrice?' Charlotte asked her, once. 'Anything at all about the other side?'

'Well, I thought I did to begin with. It was all so very clear . . .' said Beatrice. 'But then came the fog. The creeping black fog inside my head. Mixing it all up. Making everything more and more vague until . . . until now, I'm not so sure. What little there's left doesn't seem very real any more.' The peculiar, impenetrable way she was looking at us, made me wonder if she wouldn't rather not remember. As if it was all just too painful.

I found myself nodding at her in agreement, or at least in understanding, and Charlotte nodded too, her tears beginning to fall. I think if we were honest, it was the same for us all.

It was only then that I realised the elusive Mildred had crept up on us, unnoticed. The old ghost cat always did appear when she was least expected. She was standing at the top of the stairs, and if I didn't know better, I'd have said she was listening to us. There was a strange look in her eyes that startled me. It was a *follow me* look. A *follow me if you dare* look. I've seen it before in the eyes of excited boys; when they want you to go somewhere secret, somewhere you're not allowed to be. Perhaps I should have taken more notice of her, but I didn't, not then. She only went away again.

And so . . . That's how things stayed for a while. Easy, and happy in their own peculiar way. Nothing would ever compensate me for being dead. Nothing ever can. But at least I did have friends, family almost – what with Mr Tuddle and the Pattinsons, Charlotte and Beatrice. Especially Beatrice. And maybe my death could have gone on like that forever. (However long forever was?) Which might not have been so terrible. But in the end, it didn't . . .

You see, the caller came back again. The caller at the front door.

TEN

Tap, Tap, Tap

I was alone at the bottom of the stairs. Everything was so quiet and peaceful. If I listened really carefully, I could hear the house murmuring pleasantly with the sound of ghosts content at their haunts.

It was then that it happened. Without warning.

Tap, tap, tap. Tap, tap, tap.

There was no mistaking that knock.

Tap, tap, tap. Tap, tap, tap.

What would you do if fate came calling?

All my fears, my hopes, my unanswered questions came scurrying back to me. Could it really hurt to open the front door to the knockers? What if Mr Tuddle was mistaken about the dangers of the outside world? What if these knockers weren't a threat at all? What if they'd come to help us? Maybe they had found answers to the questions he could only ponder in his papers and his journals? After all, he was only a house ghost. He had said as much himself. What did he really know for certain?

Tap, tap, tap. Tap, tap, tap.

I tried desperately hard to ignore it. What I didn't know couldn't harm me. Then again, what I didn't know couldn't do me any good, either.

Forgive me. I couldn't help myself. I crept slowly towards the front door, and listened . . .

Silence.

There was nothing to hear. Perhaps the knockers had already given up and gone on their way? It was almost a relief.

I lifted a hand towards the door catch. Hesitated. Took hold. Hesitated. I began to turn the handle—

'Edward. Please, no!' Behind me, somewhere, Beatrice was pleading. 'Please, don't do it!'

Too late. The door creaked open on its hinges.

Faint trails of spectral-light bled out into the darkness, only to fail and get lost there. Surely, if there was a street outside, *if there was*, it was empty?

'Edward?'

'It's all right, Beatrice. There's nothing here. There's nobody here.'

Then I changed my mind. There *was* someone there. Someone or something, standing before the open front door. I had the vaguest of notions: were they smiling at me? Then they spoke.

'Spare a drop of precious for a poor old ghost, dearie?' The voice might have belonged to an old woman – the ghost of an old woman. It sounded fragile and slight, and yet, there was a dark inner strength to that voice which was strangely unsettling. I felt as if a ghostly wind had just blown across my grave.

The figure held up a transparent hand to a transparent face. There was almost nothing there. Almost.

'Sorry, I . . .' I felt both guilty and threatened at once. I had meant to quickly close the door again, and yet . . . Wasn't this ghost, this poor spirit only asking for my help? She needed my help and surely, there *was* a way I could give it.

Unwillingly my hand began to move towards her. Yes, I could help her. I could help her, if I wanted to.

Suddenly, Beatrice was there next to me. Shouting, 'Edward! Edward! No! You can't!' She took hold of my outstretched hand and began to pull me inside. 'Please, quickly— Come away! You must come away.'

I tried to turn around. But as I moved, so too did the figure at the door. Before I could close it, her foot was inside. Whatever I'd begun there, it wasn't about to be stopped.

There was a ferocious rush of wind. A wuthering gale. Then the house was suddenly full of marauding ghosts, sweeping in through the open front door. Accomplices to the old woman, they had been out there with her. They had been skulking in the darkness, waiting for their moment. And now it had come.

I heard Beatrice cry out, 'Afrids—' But that was all I heard. We were instantly surrounded and I lost both sight and sound of her. I did not see her again until it was all over. All over and done with.

I was driven back along the hallway, pushed against the stones of the ancient Roman wall, suddenly in a most desperate fight. I was outnumbered, overpowered, and without the means of fighting back because I did not understand who I was fighting.

What words can truly describe what happened to me there?

Three Afrids came at me together, reaching out towards me. Grasping. But not only with their ghostly bodies. Oh no. This was to be as much a battle of wills as it was a physical fight. And I knew what it was they were after ... My Essence. My Essence of Being. Already I could *feel* the weight of their minds, pressing in upon mine. And as much as I tried desperately to hold my frail spirit body together with my thoughts, they began to tear it apart with theirs! As one, the Afrids fed. They used their combined mental strength to overwhelm my thoughts, until ... Until, I just couldn't think at all – couldn't think myself together under the menacing onslaught. I saw the sticky-tacky liquid gather and drop in long looping trails from the ends of my fingers. I saw the Afrids greedily scoop it up again. Into their hands. Into their mouths. Any way they could. Taking the precious liquid Essence that was all, everything of the ghost I'd become.

I was not their only victim.

Even as I struggled against them I heard the cries of anguish from upstairs, where an even greater battle was being fought out. Was that Charlotte, in the bathroom? Or was that Mr Andrews? Then a deafening thud, as if something very heavy was being turned over, and with great ease. A bed? A desk? Glass broke. Wood splintered with a terrifying crack. Children screamed, wailed piteously, and then fell suddenly, sharply silent.

And in among it all, there came laughter. Heartless. Cruel. Laughter that scorned.

What saved me then from a certain end, was little more than an accident. I was not long dead. A new ghost and fresh with it. Perhaps my strength of will was greater than the Afrids had expected? I'd never stopped struggling – mind or body. Somehow, I found myself between the Afrids and the dining-room door, just as the door flew open. Just as the Pattinsons came charging out in full cry. I fell into their room. The three Afrids fell with me. That was their mistake. Their attack on me had been interrupted. Between them, they had not yet taken in enough Essence to give them the bodily strength to match such an angry Kindred Spirit.

'At them now, Mother!' cried Mr Pattinson. 'At them! And don't spare the rod!'

The Afrids took off. Quickly turned and fled for the open door with the Pattinsons in hot pursuit.

But that was not the end of it. Still groggy from the attack, I found myself at the bottom of the stairs. There were more Afrids on their way down, reeling like drunks. What had taken place upstairs? What had they done there? What evil, unspeakable thing had they done?

As vile as they had first appeared, the loathsome way they looked now made it hard to even imagine these were the same creatures who had forced their way into the house. For all I knew, it was the spectre of the old woman who led them down the stairs – though there was nothing of that slight, wraith-like figure I had met on the doorstep to recognise her by. They were all of them, bloated. Their bodies glistened in a sickly way. Their faces were swollen and great gobs of liquid dribbled from their mouths. I did not need telling what it was. The sticky-tacky liquid hung from their noses like a bad cold. It sweated from their brows. It dripped from the tips of their fingers. It splashed against the walls and the floor and stuck there. And no jeering Afrid bothered to gather it up again. They only laughed and mocked the more, and left the sticky puddles where they formed. If it reminded me of anything – colourless as it was – it reminded me of blood.

Fortunately – for me – these Afrids were by now well gorged and stupefied with it. There was to be no more feeding. One by one, they staggered, ungainly, out through the open front door and were lost to the darkness outside.

The last I heard of them was a mocking cry. 'Spare a drop of precious for a poor old ghost, dearie?' Then they were gone.

'Quickly now, Edward. Quickly close the door, lad!' called out Mr Pattinson.

I was moving before he'd finished. I clashed the door shut and turned to look for Beatrice.

I found her lying on the landing floor. Where she had

fallen, I could see little more than a tattered rag.

'Beatrice?'

She did not move.

'Beatrice?'

She lay there as still as a body in death.

PART TWO
EDWARD ON THE OUTSIDE

ELEVEN

The Silence of a Memory

A sad house. A gloomy house. A desolate house. A still and a silent house.

Not the silence of death, but the silence of absence. Not the silence of hope, but the silence of a memory. Not the silence of a ghost, but the silence of emptiness.

Not that the house of the humble dead was empty of ghosts. Real or imagined.

How long had it been since the desolation of the Afrids? Time without a measure, without a reckoning, is no time. Or should that be eternity, perhaps? Ah yes, eternity. If only . . .

I was in my place at the bottom of the stairs.

In the dining-room the Pattinsons were sitting around their table, eating Sunday dinner perhaps.

In the bathroom Charlotte stood vacantly at her mirror, tears spilling down her cheeks.

In her private corner on the landing, Beatrice sat upon her stool and nursed her wooden toy.

While in some secret place, unseen and unheard,

Mildred the cat prowled endlessly backwards and forwards. Backwards and forwards.

Ghosts then, still at their haunts. Though only just. The flimsiest, the faintest, the weakest of spectres you can imagine. Like the most distant of old memories, like the wind-blown smoke from a dying chimney fire. Of course, some of us had suffered more than others at the hands of the Afrids, and perhaps poor Beatrice most of us all. Indeed, how was it that her ghost still survived? She had become so terribly, terribly frail. You would have to look hard, and it would take a well practised eye, to find her there at all.

But wait—! A word of warning here, and it's a bitter word – before we lose ourselves in self-pity. These poor, these tragic ghosts – and I number myself among them – we were the lucky ones. Yes, the lucky ones.

Please, don't go into the bedrooms looking for Mr Andrews dressed in his pyjamas and silly tin hat. His bed has not been slept in. In all his death he had never risen from that bed; now he never would.

Stay out of the nursery where among lost souls the sad ghosts of young children once idly played.

And leave the office door well alone. And the strewn papers that lie upon the desk and upon the floor there, leave them undisturbed. Especially, don't go looking for Cornelious Tuddle. Don't. Because you will not find him.

You will not find any of them. They are not there.

They are not there.

I had been too curious. *I* had opened the front door. *I* had allowed the Afrids to come inside. It was *my* fault. It was all *my* fault!

Rules are rules; in death, just as in life. And it's only when rules are broken – yes, and broken beyond repair – that you begin to see just how precious they are. Why had I not listened to Mr Tuddle? Oh, why?

The house without him felt as empty as a tomb. Like a ghost without a soul. And everywhere the spectral-light shone dimmer, yes, or ceased to shine at all.

It became increasingly difficult for me to sit contentedly at my haunt. Though neither could I face the make-believe jollity of the Pattinsons. The Kindred Spirit, who now seldom strayed beyond their dining-room. Who hid themselves away, pretending nothing had changed.

Oh, but it *had*.

More and more I found myself drawn to Charlotte and to poor Beatrice (or rather, to the poor pitiful creature she had become).

We began taking aimless walks together, the three of us wandering slowly about the house. Most often we walked in silence. Never speaking, in case the words we spoke were too sore, too deep for an already open wound. It was enough for each of us to know that the others were there, and we were all grateful for the company. (Now it seemed we were the sad lost souls.)

We would always stop just outside of Mr Tuddle's office door and gather in a huddle there. Though we would never quite dare to open it and go in.

Once, as we walked, I broke the silence and asked a question that had been stuck inside my head ever since the loss of the others. 'Do you think death has any real meaning to it?'

Charlotte and Beatrice only looked at me puzzled.

'When I was alive, people were always asking about the meaning of life,' I said. 'So . . . Why do you think we are here, now? Surely, there has to be a point to it? It can't just go on like *this* for ever!'

'Not for ever, Edward,' said Charlotte.

We had been walking. Now Beatrice stood still, and as she did so, all but disappeared. She was so desperately frail.

I thought to myself, how little can there be of any ghost before they . . . before they . . . I was certain a single sigh would be enough to blow her clean away.

'No. I'm sorry. You're right, Charlotte. Not for ever,' I said. 'It's just that I don't think I can bear much more of this—'

'Some ghosts don't know when they're well off,' said Beatrice, in a voice as quiet as a kiss.

I closed my eyes, stopped looking at her.

My mind was made up. There was something I could do to help her. Inside my head I began to let go – you know – I stopped thinking-myself-together-with-my-thoughts. It came surprisingly easy. Almost instantly I felt the first slight sticky trickles spilling out into the palms of my hands. I opened my eyes. I held out my hands towards Beatrice.

'Here. I want you to have this. Go on, take it.'

'What?' Beatrice began to back away from me.

'Please? It's mine to give you. And I want you to have it.'

'No, Edward. No. I can't. I just can't.'

'What do you mean? Why can't you? Just take a look at yourself. Why can't you? I did that to you. *Me*! What else have I got to offer?'

Beatrice was still backing away. 'Edward, you can't offer me anything. I don't want it. When it's done with, it's done with. When it's finished it's finished! Don't you see? Nothing lasts forever. That's just the way it is.'

'What— ? You mean, fwut. Just like that? Fwut – and it's all over.'

'Yes. Just like that, Edward. And for all of us.'

'Like Mr Andrews? Like those children in the nursery?'

'Yes.'

'And Mr Tuddle, too?'

'Yes, Edward, Mr Tuddle, too. Yes! Yes! Yes!'

She tried to turn away, but I wasn't ready to give up.

In earnest, I held out my hands again, deliberately putting them in her way. The few sticky drops of pearly liquid shone like jewels on the ends of my fingers. Beatrice only moved around them. And as she did, she seemed to drift away along the landing – leaving little more than the flimsiest trail of spectral-light behind her.

I think that was the darkest, the saddest moment I have ever known.

'Beatrice?' I called after her.

'Let her go,' said Charlotte. 'Leave her be.' I'd almost forgotten about Charlotte. She was gently stroking Mildred, who had slunk up the stairs unnoticed. Mildred . . . I remembered the circumstances of my death, when the ghost cat had cheekily helped herself from my sticky-tacky puddle. Could I condemn her for simply having the instinct to survive?

'Cats will be cats,' said Charlotte, as if she was reading my thoughts. But then she added something that fairly shook me. 'And Beatrice *can* be Beatrice. If you really want?'

'What?'

'Why do you think she won't take your Essence from you? And I notice you never offered me any?'

'I don't know— What? Oh, I'm sorry, I never thought—'

'Forget it, Edward and listen. Look, she *likes* you. I like you if it helps any. She won't take it off you because its yours. It might do her some good, but it would only hurt you. There's none of us with more Essence than we need. And once it's all gone, it's *all* gone . . .'

'Oh, but you just said—'

'I said, listen. The Professor wasn't perfect, but he was right about a lot of things. There *are* Afrids outside who would steal your Essence of Being. We know *all* about them — and only too well!' She paused, briefly. 'But Edward, there's more . . . Where there are thieves to steal there are always hawkers to buy back from.'

'Eh?'

'Hawkers — street-traders. Rogues. What can be stolen,

can as easily be bought and sold. All we've got to do is make a trade with them. Beatrice can hardly argue about Essence that comes from a fair trade, now can she?'

'But outside?'

'Yes. Outside.'

'But how do you know?'

'I know—!'

I looked at her hard, but she wasn't giving anything away.

'You've been on the outside, haven't you, Charlotte? But the rules—?'

'Oh, Edward! Did you think you were the first ghost ever to be curious about what goes on, on the other side of the front door? Yes, I've been outside.'

'And the hawkers? . . . You could take *me* to make a trade with the hawkers?'

She didn't answer directly. 'Edward it's not easy . . .'

'Easy?'

'We're house ghosts. Ghosts are meant to stay where they belong . . . The Professor was right about that too! I, I'm not sure if I'm strong enough to go outside again. You know—?'

'Oh.' I didn't really know, but I nodded all the same. I'd been so wrapped up with Beatrice's plight I was forgetting we'd all suffered at the hands of the Afrids. We could all do with some help.

'I could probably tell you how to reach them, though. If you want to try . . . ?'

'I want to try, Charlotte.' I said, hesitating. 'There's

just one thing. What have I got that's worth trading with hawkers?'

Charlotte tutted lazily, more like her old self again. 'Use your noggin, Edward. Everything's got a value to some ghost – especially when it's rare. Think about all the stuff we bring with us when we die.'

'You mean our manifestations, objects and that?'

'Exactly. You can't get much rarer than those, can you?'

'Yes but, hawkers are hardly going to be interested in my Guy Fawkes, or our Aggie's fluffy slippers, now are they?'

Charlotte tutted again. 'Come on, that's easily remedied. Follow me.' She was looking at the closed doors along the landing.

'What? You don't mean—'

I'm not proud of what we did next. Then again, haven't you ever done anything you weren't supposed to? Don't expect me to turn into a perfect little angel just because I'm dead. It doesn't work like that. Anyway, it might please you to know I still feel guilty about it, and I can hardly bring myself to say it, though there are plenty of names I could use. Thieving, robbery, burglary, any one of them would do. Or maybe the phrase I'm really searching for is grave robbing, because that's how it felt to me.

Together, Charlotte and I went into the empty bedrooms (though I'll not tell you which). We took a pocket watch from a bedside table, and a carriage clock from a desk. From a bookcase we took both a silver inkstand and books – though not too many books. You see, whatever we took then, I would have to carry outside with me later.

Oh, and of course, we didn't tell anyone else what I was planning to do. Ignorance is bliss. We left Beatrice sitting on her stool, nursing her wooden toy, and the Pattinsons at their table eating Sunday dinner.

TWELVE

The Ghost Town

Go on then, Edward. Go on, Edward Gwyn Williams. Do it, if you're going to.

I was standing behind the front door with my hand on the latch, trying desperately to pluck up the courage to open it.

'You don't have to, you know,' said Charlotte, at my back. 'Nobody would think any the worse of you if you didn't—'

'*I* would,' I said, snapping at her. Though I hadn't really meant to. It was myself I was annoyed with. '*I* would,' I repeated, more softly. Then, at last, I did it. I turned the latch on the door.

When the lock gave way under my hand and the front door creaked open on its hinges I gasped involuntarily, and took an unnecessary deep breath. What was I expecting? The Afrids to come charging in through the open door to finish us off? Well, they didn't.

Nothing happened. Nothing moved. There wasn't another sound.

I gave a look back across my shoulder. Charlotte was beginning to cry again.

'You'll remember the things I've told you, Edward?'

I gave a shrug, and half nodded with it. What difference did it make if I remembered or not? I knew I was going to go outside anyway. And Charlotte's instructions weren't exactly clear. It turned out she had only ever been on the outside once. (I think once is usually enough for any house ghost.) She'd even written me out a list, but there were no proper directions. No, take your first left, second right, first left and then keep straight on until you see a sign that says hawkers. No. It was more a case of any way the wind blows you.

1. Keep your eyes wide open.
2. Don't talk to any strange ghosts.
3. Watch out for recognisable landmarks (to follow on the way back). And—
4. You'll definitely know the hawkers when you run into them.

Do you see what I mean?

Quickly — as if quickly made it easier to do somehow — I slipped out through the open door. Behind me, Charlotte pushed it closed — *click!* No going back now.

On the doorstep I stopped, and just stood there. I don't know what for, I just did. I was holding my various trades in my arms, hugging them tightly together, like they were a pack of tiny pups saved from a drowning.

What struck me first about the outside, was that it did

not *feel* like outside. It was an empty cavernous stretch of nothingness, only marked where distant pale clusters of spectral-light – far out of reach and unfathomable – stained its very blackness grey. But it was a vacant, a weather-less void, without heat or cold, without wind or rain to define it.

And please, don't ever ask me to draw you a map of it. I can't do it. The outside world of the dead doesn't work like that. It doesn't really start anywhere or finish anywhere. It's just a sort of somewhere among a vast nowhere. And if that sounds vague and unhelpful, tough, it's the best I can do. You try getting anywhere using Charlotte's feeble instructions.

Around me, my own spectral-light began to gather. There were no walls here for it to cling to, no familiar staircase or furniture to wrap itself around. Slowly it crept out into the darkness ahead of me, searching there for a path it might mark out, a path I might follow.

Cautiously, I began to move. I took a step, and then I took another step.

The darkness stayed silent, and more importantly, it stayed empty. How far would I have to go to find what I was after? I did not know.

Another step. And another.

Soon, I became aware that I was walking upon paving stones. Oddly, that made me feel uneasy. Maybe I was getting worried about where the path might be leading?

Then I began to sense something else, close by. Something else, standing out there in the darkness.

It wasn't a person or an animal ... It was a building. A house? Yes, another house.

There was no light, no spectral glow to mark it out. Only the physical weight of its presence; heavy and brooding. If there were doors, if there were windows — which I could not see — I just knew they would be standing open. Not as an invitation, but as empty gaping holes. This house was no more than a desolate stone shell. It was a haunt long since deserted by any ghostly inhabitants. Whatever had gone on here it was a thing finished with. And the house did not want reminding of its past. Even my own spectral-light was reluctant to touch the face of its stone walls.

I hurried on past. And as I did, something fell from my grasp and got lost in the dark there. Was it the pocket watch? I didn't stop to find it.

I began to follow a stretch of road that led eventually to more houses. A short terrace of three this time. They were numbered; thirty two, thirty four and thirty six. But why were they here, standing out on their own? I went up close, at least I went up as close as I dared. I couldn't see much, but there were long strips of sticky tape criss-crossing all the windows, and behind them heavy black curtains that reminded me of Mr Andrews' bedroom. That's when it clicked. They were blackout curtains. World War Two blackout curtains. And three houses together? That's just how it was. Whole families, whole rows of families blown to bits by a falling stick of bombs. In life there was probably nothing left. They'd have built posh new houses on the site after the war, or maybe made a playing field for the local kids to muck about on. But here, in the world where the dead belonged, the three bombed houses stood resolutely intact. There were thin grey threads of smoke coming from their chimneys, and through a slight chink in the curtains I could see the friendly glow of spectral-light. I was almost sure I could even see shadows moving, and hear the faint sound of music being played on a piano.

My mood lightened a little, but I didn't dare stop. Not yet.

I had to skirt around the edge of the garden at number thirty six to get any further, because I suddenly came up against a steep bank of solid nothingness. And coming through a gap in a hedge I found myself facing a car that was sitting sideways across a short stretch of narrow road (too short to lead anywhere). The car was lit up by a vaporous trail of spectral-light dripping from a single street lamp. I could make out two ghosts sitting in the front seats.

I tried to smile at them, and I waved, but the driver only turned angrily away and yelled, 'Go away will you! Won't anyone ever just leave us alone! Go away!'

I found myself running, until the car was out of sight.

The next ghost I met was a horse standing out in an open field. It let me feed it grass from my hand, nuzzling me in a friendly way, as if it had not done so in a very very long time. I should have realised, when you're dead nothing is quite as it seems. I began to feel the weight of the creature's thoughts . . . How lonely, how desperately lonely this poor ghost was. The horse wanted me to stay there with it. It wanted me to stay in that field, for ever.

I pulled away from it and quickly moved on.

Then, suddenly, I was passed by a youth who was riding a bicycle. He was wearing a jacket and a scarf and a flat cap, that all seemed far too big for him. He rang his bell loudly and gave a cheery, 'Good mornin',' as he went by. He disappeared as quickly as he'd come. He vanished into the darkness behind me and I never saw him again.

There was a brightly lit corner shop (though missing most of its street). Behind its huge plate glass window there were neatly stacked towers of tinned food with hand-printed cards announcing extra special offers. There were garden peas for sixpence a tin, and carrots for twopence ha'penny. And a large smiling poster explained, IT'S ALL AT THE CO-OP, NOW!

I peered in through the window, past the displays. There was a big polished wooden counter. And behind it there was a smartly dressed grocer, in a white coat and with a sharpened pencil tucked workmanlike behind his ear. He was smiling, passing the time of day with two elderly women. Every so often he would turn to the shelves behind him and lift down a large packet or a glass jar, and carefully spoon out a measure into little blue or brown bags.

Something made me want to go into that shop, though its door was shut and I knew that I couldn't. I even took hold of the handle. In the end though, I remembered Charlotte's instructions and I let it go again. This was not my haunt. This was not where I was going, not this time.

I might have been keen to avoid the Afrids and I wasn't exactly looking forward to meeting up with the hawkers, but I had to get on.

Sometimes I passed large clutches of houses, tightly packed together. Sometimes there was only road, bare and dark and desolate. More than once the road fell away to a dirt track and then there were houses that were nothing more than huts, without proper windows and with straw roofs. They reminded me of drawings I'd once seen in a school history book. Sometimes there were men outside the huts, and sometimes women with animals. There was a young boy tending pigs inside a wooden enclosure. The stink was overpowering. That came as quite a shock. It was the very first thing I had smelled since the moment of my death.

The pig boy looked at me without expression as I passed him. He did not need a door to keep our ghosts apart. The sheer weight of his spirit, his overpowering strength of will was a far better barrier than any lock or key could ever be. I was sure no prowling Afrid would ever bother this ancient ghost.

I kept walking.

There was another desolate house. And then, of all things, a church – with a vicar standing in the open doorway. This time when I waved, the ghost waved back, but still I wouldn't stop. I wasn't on my way to church.

The path I was walking on narrowed there, and ran up against the edge of a wall that enclosed the churchyard. That was another surprise. There wasn't a single ghost among the gravestones. Of course – I worked that puzzle out for myself – people are already long dead before they're buried in their graves. The one place you're guaranteed *never* to find a ghost is in a graveyard.

Buildings began to grow up around me thick and fast. Almost before I knew it, I was in the middle of a town. And a ghost town? Yes, of course a ghost town. What else? I could hardly believe my eyes. This was no kind of town I had ever seen before.

Whole buildings, whole streets loomed before me. They criss-crossed each other, criss-crossed again, growing in and out of each other until they were so hideously misshapen, it was impossible to tell one from another. Where two buildings sprouted from the same piece of ground, they wrapped themselves together, rather like an awkward pair of youngsters having their first snog. They spiralled upwards, out into the darkness, teetered gingerly there (always on the point of, but never quite collapsing).

And ghosts? To my utter amazement the centre of the town was a bustling sprawl, a hive of noisy activity. There were ghosts everywhere! And all shapes, all sizes. Terribly ancient ghosts and frightfully modern ghosts. The ghosts of tiny children and the ghosts of boisterous teenagers. The ghosts of granddads and grandmas. Some ghosts stood boldly alone, strong and confident free spirits going about their business unhindered. While other ghosts walked warily, with their heads down, but their eyes ever watchful. Many were Kindred Spirits, like the Pattinsons, finding safety in numbers.

And with so many ghosts together in one place the spectral-light blazed brightly. It burned like a furnace, pushing the darkness out to the corners of the streets, and into grim back alleys, where the brooding Afrids were left to loiter. Ah yes, there *were* Afrids, obvious with their obscene bloated bodies, even in the shadows. Perhaps they were hoping some lone, weary ghost would take a wrong turn, get itself lost and wander their way so they could set upon it? (Certainly, they weren't being as brave, as openly fearless as the last time I'd seen them — not now they were faced with more than a few simple, unsuspecting house ghosts.)

And if there were thieving Afrids about, then surely there were hawkers, too? Isn't that what Charlotte had said? Wherever you find one, you're bound to find the other?

I looked towards the very darkest of the dark alleyways. Charlotte's instructions were plain enough. I would know the hawkers when I found them. Well, I had found them . . .

THIRTEEN

The Hawker

'Are ye buyin'? Or are ye sellin', lad?' a suspicious voice hissed drily. It spoke the instant I stepped out of the light of the street and into the darkness of the alleyway. I almost drew back into the light. I had to force myself to stand my ground.

'Eh?' I squinted, tried to see who was there. It had sounded like a woman's voice. But there was so little spectral-light, and it was murky and feeble, and clung like a shroud to the very edges of the alleyway, making the darkness behind it seem even more dark.

The voice did not repeat itself.

'I'm— I'm buying,' I said, trying not to sound nervous. Silence. Then—

'Come thee here then, my pretty pet. Sit thysel' down at my table, and mek it fast. What have ye got that's worth the takin'?'

'Taking?'

'Slip o' the tongue, lad. Beggin' your pardon. Now, sit thysel' down and mek thy trade.'

I edged a little further along the darkened alleyway. There really was a table there – or at least, a box or crate serving the purpose – and there was a cloaked figure sitting behind it. Though neither were more than vague silhouettes.

I set the books, inkstand and clock down on the table. As I did the clock chimed, just once. Its sweet silvery tone sounded desperately out of place but it was enough to distract the hawker. She began greedily fingering the objects, hissing and sighing with a kind of sickly passion.

After a few moments though, she appeared to lose interest.

'What's all this, then?' she hissed in a carefully practised manner, sliding the objects (albeit gingerly) back across the table towards me. 'Ye playin' me games, my pretty pet? What would I be wanting with the likes o' these worthless trinkets?'

'They're not worthless,' I said, hoping that her sudden loss of interest was only part of her act. 'They're books. You could try reading them. And you can tell the time with a clock.'

'Tah! What kind of a nonsense—! You'll have me swearin' politely on me fetha's grave and all.' The hawker suddenly leant against the table and pushed it away. She stood up and stepped further back into the darkness, as if she meant to leave.

'No, wait! Please, wait! We have got something more. Look! It's jewellery!'

The voice came from behind me, and I knew it at once. I couldn't believe it, but I definitely knew it.

'Charlotte! What on earth are you doing here?' I cried.

'I followed you, didn't I. I couldn't let you come on your own—'

'You *followed* me . . . All this way?'

'Now then, lad,' interrupted the hawker. 'Have ye business to do here? Ye or thy lassie? Or am I best on my way?'

'Yes, we have business!' said Charlotte. Something flashed brightly in the palm of her hand. 'Here, take *this*! Take it along with all the rest. This is our trade.'

She was holding out a ring.

'Along with *all* the rest, ye say?' Greedily, the hawker snatched it. 'Well now, isn't this a pretty piece!'

'But Charlotte, you can't!' I cried. 'That's your engagement ring. It's all you've got left to remind you—'

'She already has, my pretty pet,' laughed the hawker. 'It were hers freely given. And now it's mine, freely taken. Them's the only rules in this world.' The hawker seemed well satisfied with her trade. She quickly slipped the ring out of sight and pulled the clock, inkstand and books close to her across the table.

'So, which of ye is it to be then?' she asked. 'Who's after takin' my own sweet precious?'

I looked towards Charlotte. 'It was more your swap than mine . . .'

Charlotte shook her head. 'You take it Edward. I don't think I can.'

'Be makin' up your minds,' hissed the hawker. 'It's not like we've got forever to wait, now is it?'

For the first time spectral-light began to creep tentatively around her form, highlighting her hooded face. She was the most ancient creature I think I've ever seen, alive or dead! What slight features she had were all but lost among the wrinkled parchment that passed for skin. Only her eyes shone, and those were like cold, brittle shards of ice.

'All right,' I said, not quite daring to look straight at her. 'All right. I'd better take it.'

The hawker rolled up her sleeve and laid a pale withered hand flat down on the table. She narrowed her eyes, without quite closing them, as if she was thinking . . . or rather, more accurately, as if she was trying *not* to think. Slowly, ever so slowly, a small pool of glowing liquid began to form on the table top.

'There now, lad.' The hawker opened her eyes. 'There it is. And ye'd best take it quick, afore I change my mind.'

'Is that it?' cried Charlotte. 'Is that all you're giving us for a diamond ring? For everything?'

'It's a seller's market, dearie. Let the lad take it or leave it. It's all the same to me. The dealing's done!'

'But that ring is *real*!'

The hawker was suddenly cackling. 'Ye are dead and buried in thy grave, dearie. Nothing is real!'

'And how come you've got so much that you can afford to give it away?' I said. 'Where does it come from?'

'It's too late to be getting thyself a conscience, my pretty pet. What is mine to trade is mine to trade, however it's come by! And who are thee, anyway? And by what right do ye ask so many questions of me? Now take your sweet precious and get thyselves gone. Oh, and do me a favour, next time ye are in the market to buy, take thy trade to some fool else!'

Before I could reply the hawker disappeared, easily losing herself in the darkness of the alleyway. The ring, the ink stand, the clock and the books all disappeared with her.

'Quickly now, Edward,' said Charlotte. 'Do as she said! I don't think we're alone here. There are sure to be Afrids lurking in the dark.'

I raised my hand above the glowing pool of liquid. I was still hesitating, doubtful. Was it stolen? And if it was, what price had some poor soul paid to give us this . . . ?

'Edward, please! Forget your conscience and think about poor Beatrice!'

'All right! All right!'

I tried to concentrate my thoughts on lifting the sticky-tacky liquid from the table, taking it into me through the very tips of my fingers. Though as it began to work, the feeling was so strong, it hurt my fingers and left me reeling. I'd forgotten just how much of my own Essence I had lost to the Afrids.

'Come on, Edward,' said Charlotte. 'We're going home.'

Beatrice was waiting for us when we got back to the house. She was standing at the top of the stairs and caught us as we came in through the front door.

'I know where you've been, Edward. I know what you've done. And I will not touch a drop of it. Not one single drop! Don't ask me to!'

I had never seen her look so angry. Her whole body, so thin, so transparent as it was, twisted into ugly contortions as she spoke. 'What ever made you do it? What possessed you to go outside after all that's happened here?'

'You mustn't blame Edward,' said Charlotte. 'It was my idea—'

'It was the only way we— The only way *I* could think of helping you,' I said. Though I could hardly bring myself to look at her. Every rung of the staircase showed clearly through her. I was certain she did not have long left. 'You saved my death once, Beatrice. I only thought if I made a fair trade— I thought—'

'That's just it. You didn't think, did you Edward?' Beatrice turned away, only to turn back again. 'And as for a fair trade . . . Edward, Charlotte, I will not see *murder* done just so that my death can last a few short moments longer. You must know that the hawkers find their trades among the Afrids. And you know where the Afrids find theirs! . . . Oh, how could you do it? It makes you no better than them. Don't you understand that?'

'We don't *know* that it was stolen. It might have been the hawker's own,' said Charlotte, the tears streaming down her face. 'Hers to give freely—'

Beatrice threw down her wooden tiger, not believing a

word. If it was a deliberate attempt to shut Charlotte up, it worked.

And what could *I* say? Nothing. I could only stand in silence. Being dead just wasn't turning out the way I'd expected. Now I was faced with – of all things – a ghost with moral principles. I mean, *can* you murder a ghost when a ghost is already dead?

I noticed Mildred then, sitting on the stairs close to Beatrice. She'd performed her usual trick of slipping in unnoticed. And while we argued she was content to groom herself with long slow strokes of her tongue. There was a throbbing purr lifting from her throat. That ancient cat looked so rudely fit – almost too healthy, too solid. What a contrast there was between her and poor Beatrice.

How had she managed to stay dead for so long? If only cats could talk – I found myself wishing – if only she could tell me.

Mildred stopped grooming mid-stroke, with a back leg stretched out over the top of her head. She looked directly at me. I thought for one moment she was going to say something, as if wishes can come true. Of course she didn't. There was only that strange look in her eyes. The one that said, *follow me if you dare.*

It was then that Mildred gave me her answer. Not in words, her answer was far better than any words.

'Edward? What's the matter?' said Beatrice. 'You're not listening to me, are you? And why are you looking at me like that?'

'It's not you,' I managed to say, dumbfounded. I shot a look at Charlotte; her mouth was standing wide open, though nothing was coming out. She had obviously seen it too. 'No, it's not you, Beatrice . . . It's Mildred, and your toy tiger.'

'What? What do you mean?' Beatrice looked down at her feet. 'Where's it gone? I dropped it right here. And where's Mildred? I can't see her. Edward? Charlotte?'

At last Charlotte found her voice. 'They, they've . . . they've gone!' she said.

'They've gone!'

FOURTEEN

A Matter of Possession

'Well, I can't find anything like *that!*' Charlotte had her head inside a book.

'Please, just keep looking, will you,' I said.

We were all sitting solemnly around the desk in Mr Tuddle's office, sifting through his personal papers and journals. Beatrice, Charlotte and I. Even the Pattinsons had agreed to come out of the dining-room to help. Though the Kindred Spirit was not at all happy about it.

'I'll tell you, lad,' said Mr Pattinson. 'I don't like rummaging through a dead man's privates.'

'No. It don't *feel* right. Do it Father?' said Mrs Pattinson.

'Confidentials is confidentials.' Mr Pattinson shook his head sadly, and his family shook their heads in unison.

To be honest, I agreed with them. We weren't even sure what it was we were looking for. Then again, where else were we going to find some answers?

'Hasn't anyone found *anything?*' I asked.

'Oh, there's all kinds of other interesting stuff, Edward,'

said Charlotte. 'Though I'm not *really* sure I understand it . . . Did you know the Professor had his own theories about life before death? There's even a theory here about life after death, y'know after death's end – a sort of an *after* afterlife, I think. There's just nothing here about disappearing cats!'

On close inspection, I could see that Mr Tuddle's papers were all handwritten. Even some of the printed books on the shelves around his room had had their titles scratched out and new ones written in by hand. It wasn't difficult to see why. Ever since the moment of his death, for more than a hundred years, Mr Tuddle had been writing down his theories. He'd simply run short of blank paper and started on his books. He'd written between the lines of type and down the edges of the gutters. Sometimes he had even turned books sideways and written across the existing texts.

'Oh, explain it to me again, Edward,' said Beatrice, unusually impatient.

'I've told you – it's not my fault you won't believe me. Mildred stood up. Took a quick sniff at your wooden tiger and then . . . then . . .' I waved my hands vaguely through the air.

'And then you say she climbed *inside*.'

'I don't *say* she climbed inside. That's what she *did*.'

'And then the tiger simply walked out through the wall,' added Charlotte. 'I saw it too!'

'Nothing else?' asked Beatrice.

'No! Nothing else. Isn't that enough?'

'Wait one moment!' exclaimed Mr Pattinson. His nose

was stuck firmly inside a book, while his family peered eagerly over his shoulder. 'Listen to this everyone. I think I might have found what we're looking for – if I can only make it out. It's in what the Professor called his *A to Z of Death*. There's a subtitle. *Terms and References Explained*. Here it is— *P is for Possession.*'

'Possession?' I had to interrupt. Something had jogged in my memory. I looked at Beatrice. 'Don't you remember? Don't you remember Mr Tuddle telling us about this?'

'Um . . .' Beatrice only looked blank.

'*P is for Possession*,' Mr Pattinson began again. 'And it reads thus . . .'

It has long been my profound assertion – and indeed it is a widely-held belief among the most eminent of scholars – that all ghosts (though most particularly, those of a strong disposition and with a resolute purpose of mind) are more than capable of making an actual physical possession of an inanimate object.

(Though, I feel obliged to add at once, a certain, cautionary note. It concerns the – shall we say – suitability of any given object for such an enterprising endeavour. Consider: a wise, a prudent ghost would do well to ensure that their favoured, requisite object is both similar in stature, dimension and elasticity, to wit – to themselves. Indeed, an ill-gotten match is at all costs to be avoided, and would – in all matters concerning movement and deportment – greatly restrict the abilities and freedoms of the ghost in question.)

Mr Pattinson paused there, just in case someone felt the need to interrupt again, but nobody did, so he continued.

Further (and notwithstanding my aforementioned analysis) it is my confirmed belief – made only in the light of close, personal, accurate and oft repeated scientific observation of the most diligent nature – that such a possession can, and will result in the said ghost and the said object being ejected – shall we say – from this plain of spiritual existence only to be returned to that other – shall we say – earthly-bound existence we call life! (From whence they did both, by circumstance of nature, first originate.)

Mr Pattinson stopped reading. There was a very long and thoughtful silence as we tried to take it all in, followed by a slow tutting noise from Charlotte.

'Well . . . What exactly does all that mean, when it's been walked around the houses?' she asked.

'I don't think I want to know what it means, it all sounds thoroughly disgusting,' said Beatrice.

I stood up, walked over to the corner of the room, and took Mr Tuddle's stuffed rabbit down from its shelf. 'I suppose . . . I suppose it means that ghosts the size of cats *can* climb inside of toy tigers!' I said. 'And I think the Professor has watched Mildred do it – more than once. Or at least, something just like it.'

'What, and now Mildred and the toy tiger have been catapulted back into the living world? It doesn't sound very likely!' said Charlotte. 'Isn't there something easier? Anything under D for Disappearing?'

'No,' said Mr Pattinson, 'I'm afraid not.'

'And anyway, what's the point of it all, Edward? How is it going to help Beatrice, even if it is true?'

'I don't know,' I said, raising my voice. 'I only know as much as you do!'

We all sat there, huffily flicking backwards and forwards through the pages of Mr Tuddle's journals. But nothing else seemed to help us in any way.

'So . . . What do we do now?' asked Beatrice, at last.

'Wait for Mildred to turn up again, I suppose,' said Mr Pattinson.

'What's the good in that?' I said. 'She can't tell us anything even then! I mean, she's only a cat, isn't she?'

'There is *something* we could do . . .' said Charlotte. She stood up and began to pace the room. Whatever she had on her mind, it wasn't an easy thing to say. 'Someone . . . *Someone* is going to have to follow after Mildred.'

'What? Do what she just did?' asked Beatrice, incredulous. 'Step inside my toy tiger? Or into one of those horrid stuffed creatures?'

I suppose Charlotte's idea should have sounded ridiculous to me too, only it didn't. You see, I was already remembering the odd glances, the strange way Mildred had so often looked at me. Surely, the old ghost cat had been wanting someone to follow her all along? Maybe she had something important to show us? Something that *was* going to help Beatrice, even now?

'Yes Beatrice . . . I mean, no Beatrice,' began Charlotte. 'I mean . . . I think we would need to choose something more familiar than a stuffed fox, and closer to our size – that's what the Professor seems to be telling us to do in his journal – something with arms and legs to move around on.'

'What, like a chair then?' asked Beatrice.

'No, not exactly.'

'Then like what, *exactly?*' asked the Pattinsons together.

'Like Edward's Guy Fawkes, *exactly*!' said Charlotte.

Strangely enough, there were no cries of disbelief or protests this time. Though everyone began to look around them in a most curious way. I tried to pretend I didn't understand what that look meant. But I did. We were all of us looking for a volunteer.

In the end it was down to me.

'Well, he is my Guy Fawkes.' I said. 'So . . . I'd better do it.' I tried to sound as if I meant it.

'Are you sure? Really sure? We, I, I could help you, if you like?' said Charlotte, trying desperately hard to be brave now that I had volunteered.

I never did give her an answer. But what choice did I have? I couldn't just wait for Beatrice to go off fwut! Wait to see which of us would go off next. Now could I?

I took hold of Guy Fawkes by his shoulders – or rather, by the shoulders of my dad's old jacket – and held him out in front of me. To be honest, I hadn't given him much thought, not since the day I'd died. Looking at him properly I realised, he was actually a lot taller and broader than I was. And his head, being made out of mum's old tights and stuffed full of rolled-up newspaper was rather on the big side. He had a button and a pin badge for eyes, but his nose, his mouth and his ears were only drawn on – with a fat felt-tip pen. (Though they still looked *quite* realistic, in a quirky sort of way.) At the end of his jacket arms I'd stapled a pair of woolly gloves to give him hands. His legs were a pair of my sister's jogging pants with their bottoms tied in knots to keep the stuffing in. And his feet were an odd pair of shoes that had last been used to do the gardening in.

There, it seemed to me, was the embodiment of my whole family, grinning at me with a felt-tip smile. I began to wonder if I would ever see them again. You know, for real. I tried to remember their faces. Mum, Dad, our Aggie. I couldn't. The woolly grey curtain of fog inside my head kept getting in the way.

'Are you nearly ready then, lad?' said Mr Pattinson, softly. 'Best not to go prolonging the agony, eh?'

'Yes,' I said, nodding gravely. 'Yes, I'm ready . . .'

All around me, there were ghosts watching attentively. Beatrice – poor Beatrice – looked anxious and worried, and as frail as a wisp of smoke caught in a breeze. Charlotte was in floods of tears, but there was also a sort of, excited but determined look about her. Like in one of those ancient black and white movies, where the girlfriends and the mothers have to steel themselves bravely as their hero flies off to win the Battle of Britain single-handed. I'll tell you, I didn't feel much of a hero.

There had been no exact instructions in Mr Tuddle's journals on how to go about possessing an object. He was all theory and no practice! Mildred had simply walked into Beatrice's toy tiger. I could only try to do the same with Guy Fawkes.

The Pattinsons were beginning to murmur impatiently.

'All right,' I said. 'I'm going . . .'

There was nothing else for it. I took an unnecessary deep breath, lifted a leg and lunged at Guy Fawkes – in the way of stepping into a stiff new pair of jeans.

There was no moment that I felt it happen. Not that I can recall. But I remember, I began to fall. Not to the floor. Further than the floor. And over and inwards at one and the same moment.

And with that single clumsy movement, Edward Gwyn Williams passed out of one world and into another . . .

Part Three
EDWARD ON THE OTHER SIDE

FIFTEEN

Dispossession

What was odd about it, was that I didn't feel as if I'd travelled anywhere. I mean, I didn't go on falling, tumbling endlessly through empty space, landing with a sudden bump – nothing like that. Nothing like that at all. Instead there was a strange feeling that I can only describe as . . . *solidness*. I couldn't tell where I was – I couldn't see – but I did feel definitely solid; in a very real, physical way I had not felt since the moment of my death.

And there were other odd, inexplicable sensations . . . of coming to a stop at the end of a pair of arms . . . of being on the *inside* of something – a head – a body – and knowing it. Does that make sense?

Only the feelings in my legs were vague; as if my ghost hadn't quite spread out into them yet. Or worse, as if it couldn't! Wasn't there enough of me to fill up my Guy Fawkes? Had the Afrids stolen so very much of my Essence? I shut those thoughts out of my head. Maybe, I was just out of practice – you know – at having a body for real? I'll tell you, after being a ghost, it takes quite some getting used to again (even when it is only the body of a Guy Fawkes). There's such a lot to remember. There are so many different parts you've got to get working together at the same time – and you can't leave anything to chance!

I tried not to panic. I tried to resist the temptation to move before I was sure of what I was doing. Slowly, I became aware of my *other* senses working.

First, came a muffled humming sound. Music? Yes ... There was distant music playing on a radio, and I was hearing it through the ears of Guy Fawkes. (Don't ask me to explain how, I can't, but that's the way it was.) And it was sound caused by acoustics and moving air. Not an invented, ghostly sound that I had to pretend was real, before I could hear it properly.

Better though, even than the distant hum of music, was the light that began to leak into my eyes – or should I say, *his eyes*? It was a shadowy, a gloomy light, thin and watery, but it *was* real light. Day light. Daylight, seeping into the dark space in which I found myself.

I tried not to get too excited. I tried to concentrate on seeing through the button and badge eyes of the Guy Fawkes I had surely become a part of. I couldn't see very far – not even with the help of the watery light. There was something getting in the way, close up against my face. A wall? A bare brick wall?

It was no good, I couldn't keep still any longer. I just had to know where I was.

I tried turning my head, my new, tights-stuffed-full-of-newspaper, head. I only managed to lurch awkwardly forwards. I slid down the face of the wall, causing an avalanche of movement. When it settled, I realised I'd turned over sideways. I still couldn't feel my feet or legs but I was beginning to see things more clearly.

There was an outline of a room. There were tin cans and wooden brooms. There were cardboard boxes – one with the photograph of a baby doll on it. There were odd bits of driftwood, plastic bottles draped in cobwebs, piles of old newspapers and heaps of old clothes that smelled oddly familiar.

Smelled? That was my next surprise. Miraculously, my Guy's nose was beginning to work. There were all kinds of smells. Some I'd forgotten all about (some I never realised I knew). The sweet smell of cut grass and stale petrol fumes. The dry smell of cement dust and the sour smell of rusting iron nails.

There was a sudden creak and clack and grind as something heavy and metallic was thrown open in the shadows behind me. An instant slice of bright sunlight cut through the gloom and lit up the bare brick walls all around me. I was hit by a kaleidoscope of brilliant colours. An intense, bright blue shot through with the most vivid greens and browns and reds and burnt oranges I'd ever seen.

Wasn't that the sky I could see? And the leaves of autumn trees?

Then there were excited voices, and the shadows of

two figures flicked across the wall.

I suddenly understood what it all meant. All at once the picture came together. As if I'd just found the most important piece of a magnificent jigsaw puzzle – the piece that makes sense of the whole thing.

My head was reeling. I *had* become a part of my Guy Fawkes. And I *was* lying in among a pile of junk in the garage of a house. My house. Number thirteen, City Road. There really was music playing on a radio somewhere. Outside there was daylight. And now there were two girls in here with me.

My sister – our Aggie? And Glynis Chapman from up our street?

They all belonged in the real world. The world of life, and living things. And if that was all true, then I was there too!

Excitedly – stupidly – I tried to sit up, but without the proper use of my legs I only succeeded in throwing myself against the wall again, toppling the piles of rubbish.

'What was that—?' I heard Aggie say. But that was all. Her astonished cry was cut short; instantly gone. And the brilliant day light, the garage, and the living world were gone with it. For one fleeting instant, I felt a dreadful pang of sadness at her sudden loss. But then nothing more. Nothing.

I had panicked. I had panicked at the sound of my own sister's voice, and jumped clean out of the body of my Guy Fawkes. When I came to myself, I was back where I'd begun – inside the house of the humble dead – sitting among the gloomy spectral-light at the bottom of the staircase.

Beatrice and Charlotte were standing over me. The Pattinsons were anxiously examining Guy Fawkes, tugging at his clothes, as if they needed to prove to themselves he was real.

'Oh, Edward, are you all right?' asked Charlotte. She swopped a worried look with Beatrice.

I nodded my head, stretched out my arms and my legs. 'At least, I think so.' It felt so strange, being just a bodiless ghost once more. It reminded me of that first, wobbly, heavy-but-weightless moment you experience when you climb out of a swimming pool after a long swim.

'You disappeared,' said Charlotte, 'as you stepped into Guy Fawkes.'

'Then there was nothing—' added Beatrice.

'Until we heard this horrid scream,' said Charlotte. 'And Guy Fawkes came tumbling back through that solid wall.'

'Oh, Charlotte. Beatrice—' I wasn't quite sure how to tell them. 'I've been back.'

'Back?' The Pattinsons were looking curious.

'What do you mean, back?' said Charlotte.

'You know. *Back*. In the living world. I mean back in the living world. On the *other side*.'

'What?'

'In the world of living people! In the year 2000! It really does still exist. And we can get there!'

'Oh I knew it! I always knew it!' cried Charlotte excitedly. The Pattinsons only began to look more concerned, but for one brief moment the failing spectral-light that surrounded Beatrice flashed brilliantly.

'What about the cat?' she asked hopefully. 'Did you see Mildred? Did you follow her?'

'Oh! Er . . . No! Mildred, I—' I'd forgotten all about Mildred. I saw the deep look of disappointment creep across her face. 'Beatrice, I'm sorry. It was Guy Fawkes, you see – I think he's just too big for me.' I explained the problems I'd had trying to fill him up with my weakened, my puny spirit body. 'I couldn't seem to get him to work properly, not on my own. His legs wouldn't do as they were told. They wouldn't move. At least, not at the same time as the rest of him. And I really did try.'

'Oh,' said Beatrice, sadly. My explanation hadn't helped.

It was Charlotte who came to the rescue. She was looking at the Pattinsons in a most curious, calculating way, as if she was trying to make her mind up about something (which only made the Kindred Spirit smile self-consciously). Then she said,

'We could try it *together*, Edward.'

'Sorry?' It was my turn not to fully understand.

'Isn't it obvious? If you can't manage Guy Fawkes on your own, then we'd do better to have a go between us.'

'You mean . . . Sort of like a Kindred Spirit?' said Beatrice.

'Would that work?' I asked, rather doubtfully. 'A joint Possession?'

'Aye well, it might, lad,' said Mr Pattinson, frowning thoughtfully. 'It just might.'

'Two heads are better than one, isn't that what they say?' said Charlotte. 'It's got to be worth a try!' As she spoke she was nodding. So, what else could I do? I nodded with her.

Maybe there was still hope for Beatrice yet. Maybe there was still hope for us all.

SIXTEEN

Awkward Questions

Now, Charlotte and I *agreeing* to Possess Guy Fawkes between us was one thing. Actually doing it for real, and going out into the living world together, was a more difficult proposition altogether. You see, there could be no practice, no experiments or trial runs to see how it's best done. No. There were just too many awkward questions with too few answers. We had all gathered together around Guy Fawkes, at the bottom of the staircase. And some ghosts were already having second thoughts . . .

'Supposing we do manage to get there,' said Charlotte. 'What happens if we arrive on the other side, just to find ourselves lying in among a pile of old rubbish in a garage?'

'A locked garage. With no way out, lad?' added Mr Pattinson, with a knowing nod of his head that was repeated by his entire family.

'Um . . .' I could only shrug.

'And even supposing Guy Fawkes *isn't* in the garage. How are we going to find Mildred?' asked Charlotte, pointedly.

'We don't even know where to start looking!'

'Um . . .' I shrugged again.

'And what are you going to do when you meet . . . you know . . .' Beatrice's voice trailed away to a watery whisper. '*People. Living* people?'

'Living people?' I hadn't thought.

'It's going to be almost impossible to avoid them, lad. Not in their own world.'

'We'll just have to be careful. That's all.'

'Careful? Careful, Edward? We'll be a walking, talking living Guy Fawkes. Dressed up in old rags and with a head stuffed full of newspaper! We're hardly going to blend in with the crowds, now are we?'

Charlotte had a point. I didn't bother with the shrug. It all sounded just too impossible.

'You'll have to go over at night,' said Mr Pattinson, knowledgeably. 'In the dark.'

'Aye, Father. That would be right,' agreed Mrs Pattinson. 'Ghosts always do their best haunting in the dead of the night. It's a well known fact.' As one, the Pattinsons began to smile enthusiastically.

'Yes. But how do we know when it's dark in the living world?' asked Beatrice. 'We're ghosts. None of us has got a proper sense of time. So how can we tell when the time is right?'

That took away the smiles.

'I don't know how we're going to do it,' I said, looking along the row of disappointed faces. 'Maybe we can't do any better than guess, and take our chances the best way we can. After all, if it's broad daylight when we get to the other side, we can always jump back again. You know – give up the ghost – like I did the first time. But if we don't even try . . .'

I stopped there and gave a deliberate, meaningful glance up the stairs, in the direction of the empty rooms. I avoided Beatrice. I knew she couldn't possibly last for much longer without help. But I'd made my point. And they all knew it.

That was it, then. There were no more awkward questions. It was now or never – if we were going, we simply had to get on with it.

I stood Guy Fawkes upright and leant him against the bannisters to keep him that way. I nodded towards the Pattinsons, gave Beatrice a wink. Then, I took hold of Charlotte's hand and smiled in what I hoped was a reassuring way.

Together we stepped resolutely forwards. We reached out towards Guy Fawkes, and lunged . . .

SEVENTEEN

Fireworks

I was startled by a sound. Just a sound. Nothing else.

It was the crying of a bird.

Bird song . . . It sounded so very beautiful. I'd forgotten. I didn't want it to stop. And I wanted to fly with the bird. I wanted to fly with the bird and listen to its beautiful songs for ever.

But then my first thoughts were quickly dispelled as other senses began to intrude.

Again came that peculiar sensation of solidness; of becoming a real part of something; of a body coming to a definite stop at the end of long woolly fingers.

And if there had been a bird singing, where could I possibly be? Surely, not inside a house or a garage? Not *inside* at all, but *outside*. Outside somewhere, in the open air.

I gave a start. I could feel the wind. A sharp wind blowing against my face.

Then, I heard Charlotte calling out to me. 'Edward? Edward? Where are we?' Her voice sounded vague and oddly muffled – as if she was finding it difficult to talk – though it was coming from somewhere very near.

At last I remembered . . . our Possession. Our joint Possession. Charlotte was here with me, on the inside of Guy Fawkes. Our spirit bodies were wrapped tightly together. We seemed to be sharing him between us.

How strange that was. How very strange . . . I was sure we were using his senses between us. We discovered that each of us had the use of one of his eyes, one of his ears, even half of his mouth. Yes, even his drawn-on, felt-tip mouth. Though his body wasn't quite so evenly divided. I could feel *both* of his arms, but only some of his stuffed, newspaper insides. Presumably, Charlotte had the use of his legs. At least, I hoped so!

I didn't try to answer her call.

Instead, I began to use my eye, or should that be . . . *his* eye, *our* eye even?

All around me, it was night. A dark night. Though I was looking up into a sky that was full of bright white snapping stars.

'Edward?' hissed Charlotte, determinedly. 'Will you *please* answer me . . . We're there, aren't we? We made it, didn't we? Oh, Edward . . . I can see a crescent moon!'

Still I didn't answer her. Scared that, if I did, I would break the spell that held us there together, and we would lose it all.

I stretched out my arms, in an effort to feel about me. It was obvious Guy Fawkes was lying on his back, but he wasn't flat on the ground. He was resting on some sort of a hill or a pile of junk maybe. Perhaps even the junk from the garage? I could feel it sliding about underneath me as I stretched out. Why had it been moved from the garage? Why was Guy Fawkes with it?

Out of the corner of my eye I began to notice distant street lamps and the glare of yellow light from the windows of houses. But then there was a different kind of light. A faint glow at first, and then fierce, flickering orange and yellow flames began to feather the night sky.

Charlotte gave a sudden squeak. Though I couldn't tell if it was fright or delight.

Every single star in the heavens seemed to erupt at once – shooting across the sky in violent explosions of light and colour. First there were greens and deep reds. Then a spattering of gold. Then luminous trails of blue and silver that briefly scratched out magical dancing patterns before suddenly dying. Spent. Evaporating into nothingness. Leaving the darkness whole again.

They were fireworks. *Fireworks!* And accompanying them came a heavy rattling noise, as thick as gunfire. Rat-a-tat-tat. Rat-a-tat-tat. While the air was filled with the sickly, sweet smell of burnt gunpowder.

'Oh, Charlotte! Can you see this— ?' I was hissing with excitement. 'I think it must be November fifth. I think we've come back on Bonfire Night!'

'Bonfire Night?' 'But Edward— We're part of Guy Fawkes! Don't they *burn* Guy Fawkes on Bonfire Night?'

There was a short shocked silence as the reality hit us.

I could hear people laughing and excited chatter close by.

Instant panic. We both began to move. Unfortunately, we both began to move in opposite directions. Sprawling, scrambling, I tried to use my arms to drag Guy Fawkes off the top of the bonfire. At the same moment, Charlotte tried to stand up and take a run and jump for it.

'Argh— !'

As we fell, the structure of the bonfire gave way beneath us. Carefully piled up mountains of cardboard, planks of wood, a three-legged table and a tea chest stuffed full of rags all slid awkwardly sideways.

People began to run. There were kids calling out to each other in the dark, clambering across the wreckage. Then a cry went up.

'Bonfire raid! Bonfire raid!'

'It'll be that lot from Canon Street! Trying to pinch our stuff for themselves!'

' 'S not a bonna raid, stupid. I told you— It just weren't made proper in the first place!'

'Were made proper! And anyway, let's just get it going before owt else happens!'

I tried to lift the Guy up on to his elbows. I wanted to see more clearly. I only succeeded in setting free an avalanche of old kitchen chairs, which had the kids calling to each other again.

'Watch it, stupid! You nearly had me head off with that lot!'

'Weren't me!'

'Oh aye! A bonna with a life of its own? Now, where's those matches?'

'Listen Charlotte,' I whispered as loudly as I dared. 'We'll have to try and work together. I can't pull Guy Fawkes clear on my own. He's got himself stuck somehow – and I think they're about to start the fire.'

'It's his leg – *my* leg – that's stuck,' squeaked Charlotte. 'It's caught underneath something. And, Edward – it hurts! It really *really* hurts! I know I'm a part of him, but I didn't think it was going to feel quite so realistic. Can't you see what it is?'

'Well if you can't, I can't! Can I? We're lying face down. And the Guy hasn't got eyes in the back of his head! Unless . . .' A thought suddenly struck me. As a boy – even the ghost of a boy – I could only move myself as far as my body would allow. Muscles and bones, real or imaginary, will only stretch so far. But my Guy Fawkes, well . . . he was built differently. He didn't have muscles or bones – just stuffing and cloth! Do you see what I'm getting at?

I tried turning his head first. I twisted it around as far as it would go, until it was almost facing back to front. It only brought more complaints form Charlotte.

'Edward! What *are* you doing? Stop playing silly games!'

'Actually, it's not a silly game. And if you'd stop squawking for a moment and use your eye you'd know why!'

'Oh— !'

I didn't gloat. There wasn't time. Now that the Guy's head was on backwards we could both plainly see what was trapping his leg.

There was a box, a big wooden tea chest lying on his foot. (Though I didn't bother to mention I could also see two boys out of the corner of my eye. Two boys, on the far side of the bonfire playing with a box of matches.)

'Right, Charlotte. All we've got to do now, is bend him over backwards to sit him up, then I think I can probably push the box out of our way!'

Without waiting for me, Charlotte began to heave and pull and thrash about. She didn't get us anywhere.

I was ready to give up, ready to jump myself out of Guy Fawkes, back into the world of the dead. I had to force myself not to. You see, if we ran scaredy-pants every time we hit trouble, we were never going to find Mildred. More importantly, we were never going to find help for poor Beatrice. For any of us, come to that!

'Hang on, Charlotte—! We've got to do this *together*!' I tried to sound confident. 'After three. We'll sit up – throw ourselves forwards at the same time. And Charlotte . . .' (it was too late for keeping secrets) '. . . Make it a good one. Those kids, they've set light to the bonfire.'

At the cry of, 'three!' Guy Fawkes gave a wild, juddering leap that threw him upwards and sideways, and left him twisted with his one free leg slung across his shoulder.

'Again, Charlotte! Again!'

Our second effort was worse than the first!

I'll be honest with you, it was sheer luck that our third attempt left us in a sitting position, with Guy Fawkes close enough to touch the wooden tea chest that was trapping his leg.

Unfortunately, the fire reached the tea chest just as I stretched out his woolly fingers towards it.

'Edward, can you move it – please?' cried Charlotte. Her voice sounded peculiar. Twisted. As if she was in pain, real pain, and crying real tears, not just pretend, ghostly ones. 'It's his leg, Edward. My leg!'

Flames were beginning to leap around the side of the tea chest, looking for the easiest place to take a hold, and licking lazily at the edges of Guy Fawkes' jogging pants legs. All I could do was grab hold of his legs and pull.

'Ouch! Yes – that's it! Edward, I'm free—! Quickly now, I want us to stand up. We're going to make a run for it.'

I wasn't about to argue.

As Guy Fawkes lurched forward I swung his head about, to face the front. I could feel the crumpled newspaper moving about on the inside. This wasn't a good time for him to start falling apart!

Around us, there was a frantic commotion going on. The bonfire had begun to spit and crackle and was throwing out a great fountain of fiery debris. Kids were crying. Men, yelling. Frightened women were running scared, shrieking at the very tops of their voices.

'Eeeee— look! There's someone moving about in the middle of it!'

'Don't be so soft woman, that's only the Guy!'

'The Guy is it? Then there's some daft ha'p'orth in there with it, trying to pull it out!'

'Quick now, Stanley! Fetch us a bucket of water!'

'Never mind a flamin' bucket! Fetch the flamin' Fire Brigade! Fetch the flamin' Police and a flamin' ambulance while you're on!'

At that very moment I changed my mind about being a scaredy-pants. This was a perfect place to panic, after all. So, I did.

I let go of Guy Fawkes on the inside. I gave up the ghost. Leapt clear. Fortunately, Charlotte leapt with me.

EIGHTEEN

Lies

At number thirteen, City Road, the resident ghosts were gathered together in the dining-room. We were all huddled around Guy Fawkes, who I'd sat up in an armchair. He was looking extremely sorry for himself. There were the beginnings of singe marks on both his jacket and jogging pants legs. Some of his felt-tip face had smudged into a blur, turning his toothy grin into a kind of idiotic grimace. And his head did not look quite so firmly attached to his shoulders as it had once done.

I began to tell the story of our narrow escape from the bonfire. The Pattinsons listened agog, and practically speechless (which was quite some feat for the Kindred Spirit). Charlotte, on the other hand, couldn't stop herself from bursting into tears, and visibly winced when I got to the part where we were almost burnt up in the fire.

'And what would have become of you, if Guy Fawkes had gone up in flames?' asked Beatrice, anxiously. Her weak spectral-light flickered, almost went out.

I looked her in the face. 'Oh, we were never in any real danger,' I said. That was a lie.

'Aye well, it were a brave attempt, lad,' said Mr Pattinson, thoughtfully. 'You've both had yourselves a very lucky escape and there's no mistake.'

'No mistake, Father,' repeated Mrs Pattinson. There were knowing shakes and nods of heads.

'Aye, lad. It's just as well it's done and over with. And I'm sure I'm speaking for us all when I say there's not a ghost in this house would have you go risking . . .'

As Mr Pattinson spoke I continued to look at Beatrice. She would not meet my eye. I so desperately wanted to give her hope.

'Oh, but it's not done!' I said. 'It's not over with!'

'What's that, lad?'

'Oh, no— !' I turned to Charlotte. 'We're going back. Aren't we?'

'Er, well—'

'Mildred is still over there, somewhere on the other side, and we're going to find her . . . I just *know* she's got something she's been wanting to show us. I just know it.'

I'll say this for Charlotte, she never once mentioned my lie about the danger we'd been in on the other side, or the scaredy-cat way I'd given up the ghost. She kept it all to herself, a secret between us. On the other hand . . . how were we going to find Mildred? In all the living world, how could we possibly find one small cat?

And of course, the very idea of a return visit to the other side didn't exactly fill us with excitement. We'd left in such a hurry on Bonfire Night. What would we find when we got there? We had no way of knowing how much time had passed. What if Guy Fawkes was back on the bonfire? Or worse, what if he'd already been burned to a crisp? We might not be able to return to the other side at all then!

As it turned out, our return visit began in the exact way our last one had done – with Guy Fawkes lying stretched out on his back. Only this time he wasn't in the garage of number thirteen City Road *or* on top of a bonfire. No. He was flat out on the ground, in the open air. I could already hear voices murmuring somewhere close by, but there was something else, something more immediate . . .

The sun was shining!

The sun was shining and the broad daylight almost blinded me. I had to resist the overwhelming temptation to give up the ghost right there.

Then I felt Charlotte beginning to move underneath me.

'Stop—' I hissed. 'Please, Charlotte. *Don't move*. Don't speak. Don't *do* anything.'

Fortunately, she didn't argue. In fact, she did exactly as she was told. I think she was in a state of shock. I think the daylight was all just too much for her.

I had to try and get my bearings. There was no darkness to hide behind here. There were no secret corners to lurk in. And above me only an empty steel blue sky, a hard cold winter's sun shining dazzlingly bright.

I waited for the Guy's button and badge eyes to get used to the daylight. Then, lying perfectly still, I tried to locate the owners of the voices I'd heard.

Close to, I could make out short tufts of green grass – obviously part of the ground we were lying on – though it was shrivelled and blackened at its tips. There were other things too. Odd pieces of wood and cardboard. A broken chair leg. Everything showing signs of having been partly burned up in a fire. And there was an iron rod sticking out of the ground with a blue and white tape stretching away from it, rather like a makeshift fence. The tape was fluttering slightly in the wind, but I could still read the words that were printed on it.

POLICE LINE DO NOT CROSS.

Then I heard the voices again.

'So, what's the story then, George?'

'Huh. No story, I'm afraid Arthur. Just the bloomin' left overs from a bonfire! It seems there *was* some sort of a hoo-ha last night. Some folk reckoned they saw someone clambering about in the middle of the fire, just as it was getting going. Called out the fire brigade – the coppers too. Of course, they had to put it out, spoil the kids' fun. They even fenced it off to keep them from coming back, having another go at it.'

'Don't suppose they found anything, though?'

'Nah – not unless you can count old Guy Fawkes here—'

For a moment there were two curious figures standing looking down at us.

'Aye, well . . . You'll not get much of a story out of him!'

'True, true. Come on, Arthur . . . There's no point in hanging around here. We've got a newspaper to fill, and there must be somebody out there just begging us to fill it!'

'I'll tell you what, George. We could give the council lads a call. Get them out here with their rubbish skips.'

'Try the environmental angle you mean?'

'Aye, aye, that's it . . .' The voices faded into the distance as their owners began to walk away.

What were we supposed to do now? I wasn't about to give up the ghost, but we didn't dare go looking for Mildred in broad daylight.

I decided to take a risk. Ever so slightly, and moving only the tiniest fraction at a time, I turned the Guy's head until it was facing the horizon. Not too far off I could see the outline of houses. The sun was standing low against them. All we could do was wait, and hope it fell dark enough for us to move *before* we were thrown into the back of a council truck, *before* we were carted off with the household rubbish!

Though as it turned out, we never did find Mildred.

No . . . It was Mildred who found us.

NINETEEN

Out on the Streets with Mildred

The sun hadn't quite set. Though once it had begun to fall it had rapidly disappeared behind the roof tops. A thin veil of clouds had turned the blue sky grey, and ever lengthening shadows were creeping out towards us from the distant houses. This was the gloom of the day then. That time around dusk when nothing you see is ever quite certain or clear. When mistakes are easily made.

There had been no sign of council workers, only a couple of nosey young kids who'd come wandering our way. They'd had themselves a bit of a poke about, but eventually got bored and wandered off again. Our luck couldn't last forever. When they'd gone, I made a decision.

'Charlotte?' I whispered. 'Are you OK?'

At first she did not answer. She'd not spoken a single word in all the time we'd lain there, not even tried. Then, at last she said,

'. . . I'm scared.'

'So am I,' I said, 'if you must know.' My admission seemed to help her.

'And Edward, we've been here for so long . . . I think the Guy's legs have gone permanently to sleep.'

'Look. It's beginning to get dark. We'd better make a move. See if we can't get ourselves away from here, out of sight, while there's nobody about. It's either that, or give up the ghost and go back.'

She didn't need asking twice. She began to twist and bend the Guy's legs. I began to use his arms to help sit him up.

It was then, at that very moment, Mildred found us. There she was, walking towards us through the grass, and as bold as brass. There was no mistaking her, or rather the awkward wooden lollop of the toy tiger she had become.

'Charlotte!' I cried. 'You're never going to believe this—it's Mildred!'

'What— ? Oh, Edward you're right!'

Guy Fawkes suddenly lurched awkwardly forward, stumbling as Charlotte tried valiantly to get him up on his feet. In desperation I threw out my arms, but I was grasping at thin air. The Guy tumbled back to the ground.

Before we could move again I found myself looking up into the painted wooden face of a toy. To be honest, it startled me. I could somehow see life behind those painted eyes, and although I knew it was only the ghost of Mildred, it made the creature seem deceptively real . . . almost alive. Did Guy Fawkes look that way too?

There wasn't time to ponder. Charlotte, growing in

confidence (and with the feeling returning to the Guy's legs) was already having another go at standing us up. While Mildred was giving us that look of hers. The one that said, *Follow me. Follow me if you dare.*

This time, we did . . .

At the start, I almost wished we hadn't followed her. The light was fading quickly now, and I could already see the odd distant fleck of yellow as street lamps began to switch themselves on, but it could never be dark enough for me.

Mildred hurried us away from the scattered remains of the bonfire, and deep into the shadows of the houses and a back lane.

'Faster, Charlotte!' I hissed. 'Try taking giant steps, we've got to keep up with her!'

'Yes, but that's easy for you to say!' she hissed back. 'You're not the one having to do it!'

Guy Fawkes wobbled uncertainly from side to side, before breaking into a sort of panicky, dancing quickstep.

Then, unexpectedly, we met our first person. A man, carrying an armful of packages, came walking towards us through the shadows of the back lane.

I quickly lowered the Guy's head, and kept his eyes firmly on the ground, hoping against hope that if we couldn't see him, then somehow, the man wouldn't see us!

I felt him turning towards us as we drew level. So, I spoke.

'Good evenin',' I said, trying to make sure my voice was coming out through my felt-tip mouth (and sounding passably human!) If the man looked at us then, I don't think he quite believed what he saw. He gave a stifled squeak, and quickly scampered off along the lane. It was enough to get us by on, just.

Mildred was still leading the way. To my horror, she turned out of the back lane and led us on to a front street, where the deepest shadows fell too close to the walls of the buildings, for us to feel safely hidden. She was deliberately taking us through the town, not away from it.

And suddenly there were *more* people about on the other side of the street. Another man. A pair of women. A mother with a toddler.

'Edward,' said Charlotte, 'are you sure Mildred knows where she's going?'

'No! No I'm not sure!' I hissed. 'And I said, *giant* steps, Charlotte! Definitely, *giant* steps!'

Even in the gathering darkness, I was sure people were beginning to stare! Pointing fingers. Gossiping.

'Mam, Mam! Look at the funny man!' Across the street a young, scrap of a boy was pulling at his mother's skirt, trying to get her attention.

'Eee, now have you ever seen anything like that, Emma? It's enough to give you the willies. It is too!'

'Eee, I know, Alice . . . What d'you think it is? One of them . . . *students?* I always said, they should *never* have done away with military service!'

I kept my eye on Mildred. She was walking quickly, always following the shadows of the buildings, firmly intent on her journey.

I felt Charlotte stretch out beneath me, desperately trying to lengthen the Guy's stride. We staggered, almost fell off the curb and into the road. I had to swing my arms heavily to turn him about, to keep him on the pavement. Somehow, Guy Fawkes stayed on his feet.

We quickly turned a street corner. Then another, at last leaving the gossips behind us. And we were gathering pace now. The path we were on was obviously taking us downhill. Though with so much swinging about going on, I found it increasingly difficult to keep the Guy's button and badge eyes fixed on Mildred.

She wasn't showing any signs of slowing down.

Then, at last, a piece of good luck for a change. The wind suddenly got up out of nowhere. Above us the already darkening sky turned a sombre black under a mass of gathering cloud. Spits of rain came first. Then an instant deluge. Rain, whipped into sheets by the driving wind, lashed across the pavements.

It was surprising how suddenly empty of people the streets became just because of the rain. (Only the traffic on the roads stayed the same, and it was too busy with itself to notice us.)

The rain water made Guy Fawkes soggy – and uncomfortable to be on the inside of – adding to his weight, and making him more difficult than ever to control. The rain slowed us down too – from giant steps to plodding baby steps – because Charlotte was reduced to dragging his sodden legs along the wet pavements. And where ever the water gathered around badly stitched-up seams it trickled deep down inside the Guy's body, which was the strangest feeling of all.

'Edward, I'm getting all wet!' wailed Charlotte. I thought she was crying again, until I realised it was a sort of giggly laugh. 'And ooooh— it's ticklish!'

Guy Fawkes suddenly stopped going forwards. He began jigging up and down, his legs turning him in wild, uncontrolled circles. Through his eyes the streets became a spinning blur.

'Charlotte, calm down will you! Before you run us into something!'

'I'm sorry Edward, the water just feels so-ooo funny. So, oooooh! Aaaaa—'

Guy Fawkes thumped into a lamp post and flumped awkwardly to the ground, landing in a puddle.

Charlotte was still giggling.

Ahead of us, on the path, Mildred had stopped. Oblivious to the rain, she turned her head back towards us, and gave us a very deliberate, long hard stare. In that moment I began to wonder about her. She seemed to take the living world in her stride. And yet, how had she coped? Was it easier for an animal somehow? I realised, she had her own private story, one we would never know.

Mildred waited there for us. She did not move again until we had dragged Guy Fawkes to his feet and run, as best we could, to catch her up.

From then on, Mildred stayed close, still leading the way but almost under our feet . . . Where on earth was she taking us?

TWENTY

The Stuff of Life

As we walked the rain kept falling steadily, keeping the streets deserted. The few living people we saw passed us by on the far side of the street, and they went with their heads bowed against the weather, or shielded behind an umbrella. If there was an odd curious glance in our direction, I would nod Guy Fawkes' head, or lift the collar of his old jacket as if against the intrusion. The distant onlooker would quickly drop their eyes, mind their own business, and hurry on.

Odd to say, but the further we walked the more I enjoyed it. It did not matter to me that the night had turned cold, wet and blustery. Through the eyes of Guy Fawkes the living world was so vibrant, so magical. And it was bursting with . . . Well, it was bursting with life, of course! From the shadows I watched the falling droplets of rain caught in the glow of the street lights, watched them explode into tiny silver cascades as they bombarded the wet pavements. The bare branches of winter trees, hung heavily under the weight of water yet to me, seemed to be draped in sparkling diamonds. And the wonderful smells! I'd forgotten that the rain has a scent all its own. And the damp soil. And the grass. Oh, even the fumes from the exhausts of the passing traffic smelled sweet!

I was lost in a beautiful daydream. And Charlotte was seeing the world the way I was, after all, we were using one eye each—

Charlotte!

She was calling out.

'Edward! Edward? How much further is it? How far do we have to go? My legs are getting *so* tired.'

I glanced down at the Guy's feet. Charlotte was having a real struggle, keeping them moving. She could hardly lift them off the ground.

'But ghosts don't get tired!' I gasped. 'They *can't* get tired!'

Then I realised, Charlotte wasn't the only one who was feeling tired. *I* had just gasped. You know, gasped for breath. I was breathing, for real. Or rather, Guy Fawkes was breathing for real. His chest was thumping up and down, fit to bust! I'll swear, he was puffing and panting like a steam train.

It was something I'd never imagined, never reckoned on. How long had we spent on the other side? Was it too long? Had we overdone it, somehow? Was bringing Guy Fawkes out into the living world much the same as bringing him alive? Was this what I'd seen in the painted wooden face of Mildred's toy tiger? I'll tell you, possession is one thing, but I didn't much fancy being the living soul to a worn-out old jacket and a few rolled-up sheets of newspaper. I'm ashamed to say, the idea almost made me give up the ghost, right there and then. I might well have done, too, if I hadn't been distracted by Mildred's sudden and insistent mewing.

I'd hardly noticed, but we had continued to walk downhill and away from the town. We had obviously come a very long way. I was expecting to find myself in a valley bottom, with roads and traffic. Well . . . it wasn't anything like that. In fact, I didn't recognise this place at all.

Are there some paths – even in the living world – that only the dead can follow? I think so.

Mildred had come to a standstill. She was facing a stone. A huge grey stone. Uncut, unmarked, but a towering monolith. Ancient. Immoveable. Silent.

Then I realised, there was another figure standing close by her. I knew it for what it was the moment I saw it. *A ghost*. Not a ghost in possession of an object, like us. This was a truly earthbound spirit. Though it wasn't there to spook us, or frighten us away. Rather it was a guide – I'm sure – a sentinel to *mark* our way.

There were no words spoken between us. No questions asked of it – not by Charlotte, not by me.

When Mildred began to move again, I made sure we moved with her. What distance we travelled along that last path I simply don't recall. Though I have it in mind – impossible as it might sound – that for the most part, we were neither walking in the living world, nor in the world of the dead. And what we found, when that path finally came to its end, I will remember for ever . . .

There, stretched out before us was a lake. A great lake, so deep, so vast, so strangely luminous, it almost appeared to stand off the ground before us. Its surface was a shimmer of liquid gold and silver, that sparkled and danced as if it was catching bright beams of sunlight. Except that . . .

Except that — of course — there was *no* sunlight here. No moonlight even, not a single solitary star!

Around and about us the darkness was complete and total. This made no sense.

Mildred turned to us, purring. She looked at me in that ponderous, expectant way of hers. Almost as if she was asking, '*Don't you see it, Edward? Don't you understand it yet, Edward Gwyn Williams?*'

Momentarily, I lifted the Guy's head and tried to look back along the way we had come. Behind us, there was only the blanket of darkness.

I turned again towards the beauty of that glistering lake. I tried to find something to say to Charlotte, but I couldn't. There was nothing to say, not for either of us.

I could only stand and stare at that strange apparition, suddenly aware of what I was looking at.

I *did* see it, after all.

I *did* understand.

In a way, it was so very easy to explain, so obvious. And yet—

What were we, us ghosts, with our leakiness and our sticky-tacky puddles, but the poorest remnants, the fading essence of life. This wonderful life. And here it was . . .

All that was living. All that was life. The boundless energies created and used. (Worse, created and left unused.) From the food greedily eaten off our plates, to the thoughts exploding on the insides of our heads. Such a precious gift, so often carelessly frittered away, unforgivably wasted. The living world was awash . . . I had seen it on the streets, I had felt its unique force, if I hadn't quite recognised it. From the houses and factories, from the office blocks and schools, from the libraries and swimming pools, from the people themselves it seeps out, unnoticed. It spills out freely, and is lost to them. Lost. Until it can be found again – surely here, within this great fathomless lake before me . . .

The stuff of life.

Mildred was the first to dip her wooden nose into the glowing liquid, but I wasn't far behind. There were no more attempts at explanations for Charlotte. We walked Guy Fawkes into the lake. I used the very ends of my woolly fingers to break open its dazzling surface. Like a sponge, its glowing liquid began to soak into me.

And the feeling! It was such an intense surge, so concentrated and gloriously pure it physically hurt. How can I possibly describe it? Scoring the winning goal in the school football match? Getting all the presents I ever really wanted for my birthday? Having a real looker, like Glynis Chapman from down our street, snog me at the Christmas party? None of those feelings comes close to it. Not even when you roll them all up into one.

And as for Charlotte? It left her speechless. And in tears. All she managed was a blubbery, 'Oh, Edward. It's so beautiful . . .' before she was lost for words.

TWENTY-ONE

Second Thoughts

'Urgh, Edward, I don't feel very well,' said Charlotte. 'I think I'm going to be sick!'

Guy Fawkes was lying flat out, spread-eagled on the ground again. I couldn't see anything, because I was staring up into a dark, empty sky, but I could hear Mildred's contented purring so I knew she was somewhere close by.

'Don't you dare be sick!' I said, and I meant it. 'This life stuff's precious.'

Charlotte began to giggle, as if I'd said something funny.

'What?'

'Well . . . precious life stuff, Edward. You know. It's a bit like that saying. Life is precious. I just thought—'

'Oh, yes,' I said. 'Ha ha.' Though I didn't really think it was funny, I did know what she meant.

'Seriously though, Edward, I'm sure I've taken in far too much Essence!'

'Of course you have. That's the whole point! Don't you get it? That's why Mildred brought us here. We have to have enough Essence for ourselves, and more than enough to spare. How else are we supposed to help Beatrice?'

'I know, but I'm so full I can hardly move. I think I'm going to burst. And it's already starting to dribble out in some *very* funny places.' She began to giggle again.

'Yes well, don't you dare go dribbling on me!' I scolded, but now I was giggling too. Giggling – for no earthly reason – and I couldn't help myself. Couldn't stop.

I'll swear, we were both of us as drunk as skunks. Not beer drunk. Not alcohol, or anything like that. But sort of drunk on life, I suppose. Yes, that's it. We were so full up we were stoned, intoxicated . . . drunk on the stuff of life.

And do you know something? It felt so-o good, just lying there, doing absolutely nothing. While all around us – somewhere unseen – the world, the whole living Universe, went about its business as usual, spiralling out into deep space on its way to infinity. I'm telling you. You want to fill yourself up on it sometime, while you've still got the chance!

But then came the moment when the laughing and giggling stopped.

We hadn't moved. We'd just gone quiet. Both of us thinking the same thoughts?

'What is it, Charlotte?' I asked. 'What's the matter?'

'Nothing . . . I . . . I don't know. Wouldn't it be wonderful if we didn't have to go back over . . . into the world of the dead?'

'Yeah, right. We could just stay here for ever . . . ?'

'Well, couldn't we?' Charlotte was beginning to sound serious.

You know, I think I could have given her a list as long as my arm, and it would have been full of good reasons to stay. Instead though, I made her a much shorter list. *Reasons to go back*. It was a list of just one.

'Beatrice . . .' I said.

Then, together, and without another word we let go, and finally gave up the ghost.

TWENTY-TWO

A Moment too Late

We weren't a moment too soon in returning home. No. We were a moment too late.

That's all it takes for things to go spectacularly wrong.

'Quickly, Edward!' I heard Charlotte's shocked cry as I fell out of Guy Fawkes and tumbled to the hall floor. She was already climbing the stairs before I could pick myself up and chase after her.

'Charlotte, wait for me—'

The spectral-light on the staircase suddenly dimmed to almost complete darkness.

We reached the top of the stairs neck and neck. I could only just make out the vague outline of ghosts standing at the far end of the landing. Surprisingly, Mildred was already there ahead of us. Her tail was flicking wildly and her ears were drawn flat against her head. There too were the Pattinsons, bent solemnly over Beatrice's stool.

What was wrong with everyone?

Then I saw Beatrice. She was sitting quietly on her stool,

just as she had so often done. Wasn't she? Surely, we were in time after all?

I called out her name. 'Beatrice!' But she did not move.

It was the Pattinsons who lifted their heads towards me. I had never seen them look so . . . so terribly grave. They did not speak. In unison, the Kindred Spirit turned away and drew themselves close together, as if they could not bear the agony of this scene a moment longer.

This final scene . . .

I tried again. 'Beatrice? Look. See what we've brought you.' I held open my arms. I quickly let go of my thoughts until I felt the sticky-tacky liquid begin to bleed out through the palms of my hands.

'And it's all for free!' cried Charlotte, beside me. 'Every last drop.'

'Not stolen or battered for. And there's as much as you could ever need, in all eternity! Mildred showed us where to find it.'

Beatrice remained still. Her face was raised towards us. Her eyes were wide open, and yet strangely sightless – and they were filled with such a look of dread and hopelessness – I couldn't be certain she saw any of us there.

'Don't be frightened, Beatrice. Please, don't be fright . . .' My voice trailed away. What use were words?

How fragile she looked. How terribly close to death's end. And she seemed to be so very far away. All but lost to us, lost without the strength now, without even the remnants of will to find her way back. If she reminded me of anything, it was a bubble, a soap bubble just as it's about to burst.

Gently, Charlotte knelt down on the floor beside her. There were tears in her eyes. Not fake, ghostly tears, but real tears. She followed my example. She stretched out her hands, and held them there, quivering, though not quite daring to touch Beatrice in case ... in case even the slightest touch might be too much for her failing spirit, and would break her apart, steal her away from us.

I could only watch in stunned silence.

Then Mildred was there, staring up at me, expectantly. I knew exactly what that look meant.

'Don't you understand, Edward? Don't you understand yet, what must be done, Edward Gwyn Williams?'

Mildred sat down close to Charlotte and waited. Waited for me to act ...

'This is not over with, Beatrice,' I heard my voice almost before I realised I'd spoken. How angry I sounded.

'Please— don't give up,' I whispered, as if even the force of my words might hurt her now. 'Don't go ...'

'I ... I don't think she can hear you, Edward,' sighed Charlotte.

As one, the Kindred Spirit turned to face me. Was it a look of hope ... or despair?

'I'm right, aren't I, Mildred?' (The cat didn't move.) 'This is *not* done with. It doesn't have to end here. I won't *let* you leave us, Beatrice!'

I cupped my outstretched hands tightly together, let the

sticky-tacky liquid gather into a pool there, until there was too much for me to hold and it spilled out over the top. Slipped through the gaps between my fingers.

'Here! You *must* take this from me!' I yelled. I was shaking. I thrust my open hands towards Beatrice, held them as close to her upturned face as I dared. As I did the spilt droplets of precious liquid spun through the air towards her, caught in a sudden burst of spectral-light. She did not try to take them, and they only fell, uselessly to the floor.

'Be strong! Fight back! Remember what you always told me and think about who you are! Think about Beatrice – Beatrice Tanner (1901)! And please . . . *take this from me*! It's the only way!'

'Oh, Edward! It's not going to work,' cried Charlotte. 'It's just not going to work. It's time to leave her be.'

She tried to take hold of my hands, grasping at them, as if she could stem the flow that way. As gently as I could, I pushed her away. 'It's all right, Charlotte,' I said. 'It's all right . . . It's just got to be all right.'

But what was I to do? What *could* I do?

In desperation, I reached out for Beatrice's hand. Her touch was so slight it felt as if I was taking hold of a dying breath.

Behind me, the Kindred Spirit gasped, but I did not let her go again. I held on. I cupped her hand gently between mine. Bathed it in the precious droplets of liquid Essence that still spilled from my fingertips. If only she would take it . . .

Could I see a change in Beatrice? Was there a difference? For one brief moment, from some distant place, I was certain I heard her murmur, then call out her name. Or was I only fooling myself? Had we come too late? Had she simply nothing left to hold her fragile spirit together? I looked down at Mildred who was still watching me.

Maybe the house wasn't quite so dark now. Maybe the spectral-light was glowing more strongly. It seemed to linger around our heads, something in the way of an angel's halo . . .

'It's *got* to be all right . . .'

I could not bear to see it finished this way. How could I watch poor Beatrice to the very end?

It was my turn to look away. I released Beatrice's hand.

I'm sure Charlotte tried to say something. 'Edward—' But I refused to listen.

I ran down the stairs, without looking back.

I stood in front of the hall mirror.

'It's got, *got*, GOT to be all right!' I'd meant to scream, to shout out loud, but my words would only come in hoarse, twisted whispers.

As I spoke I closed my eyes tight shut. What I couldn't see couldn't hurt me, could it? And oh, how I wished I could have stayed that way for ever.

But then, nothing lasts for ever, does it?

Finally, reluctantly, I had to open my eyes again, face the truth . . . It wasn't only my face I saw reflected in the mirror there.

'Edward . . .'

I could see Charlotte, on the stairs. I could see the Kindred Spirit.

'Edward Gwyn Williams . . .'

I could see . . .

'Beatrice—?' She was standing there, close behind me. *'Beatrice – is that really you?'*

'What *is* all the fuss about?' She spoke in such a scolding voice, but I could see she was smiling at me.

POSTMORTEM

And now . . . ?

Now, I'm sitting at the very bottom of the stairs. Beatrice is here, sitting quietly next to me, content to nurse her toy tiger. She won't say anything, don't ask her to. Though in all my death, I don't think I've ever seen her look so happy, and quite so very much like . . . Well, like Beatrice, I suppose.

Upstairs, you'll find Charlotte in Mr Tuddle's office. She's taken to sorting out his books and journals. In fact she's becoming something of a scholar (and doesn't burst into tears nearly as often as she once did).

From the dining-room I can hear the Pattinsons' happy chatter over their Sunday dinner. I expect we'll be joining them later.

Oh! And as for Mildred? Well, you might not be surprised to hear that she's disappeared again.

Things are just the way they ought to be for the dead, for the house ghosts at number thirteen, City Road.

So . . .

Is this the very end of my story, then? Is this where it all ends for Edward . . . Edward Gwyn Williams? Perhaps it is. And yet—

What with Beatrice's death saved, and all our deaths saved with it, maybe there is still hope yet for this poor ghost?

And where there is still hope, can there ever truly be an end?